OXFORD
INDIA SHORT
INTRODUCTIONS

THE POVERTY LINE

The Oxford India Short
Introductions are concise,
stimulating, and accessible guides
to different aspects of India.
Combining authoritative analysis,
new ideas, and diverse perspectives,
they discuss subjects which are
topical yet enduring, as also
emerging areas of study and debate.

OTHER TITLES IN THE SERIES

The Indian Constitution
Madhav Khosla

Natural Disasters and Indian History
Tirthankar Roy

Caste
Surinder S. Jodhka

Indian Cities
Annapurna Shaw

The Civil Services in India (forthcoming)
S.K. Das

The Right to Information in India (forthcoming)
Sudhir Naib

Trade and Environment (forthcoming)
Rajat Acharyya

OXFORD
INDIA SHORT
INTRODUCTIONS

THE POVERTY
LINE

S. SUBRAMANIAN

OXFORD
UNIVERSITY PRESS

OXFORD
UNIVERSITY PRESS

Oxford University Press is a department of the University of Oxford.
It furthers the University's objective of excellence in research, scholarship,
and education by publishing worldwide. Oxford is a registered trademark of
Oxford University Press in the UK and in certain other countries

Published in India by
Oxford University Press
22 workspace, 2nd Floor, 1/22 Asaf Ali Road, New Delhi 110002

© Oxford University Press 2012

The moral rights of the author have been asserted

First Edition published in 2012

ISBN-13: 978-0-19-808608-6
ISBN-10: 0-19-808608-3

Typeset in 11/15.6 Bembo Std
by Excellent Laser Typesetters, Pitampura, Delhi 110 034
Printed in India by Repro India Limited

To the memory of my father
P.B. Sreenivasan
and to my mother
Saraswathi Srinivasan

I shall now therefore humbly propose my own thoughts, which I hope will not be liable to the least objection.

–Jonathan Swift, A Modest Proposal

Contents

Acknowledgements

I have drawn feely and heavily on a great deal of my own previously published work, and the original sources have been cited in the text in the appropriate places. I am indebted to my co-author of an unpublished essay, Tony Shorrocks, for liberal use of parts of that essay as a basis for Chapter 2 of the present work (A.F. Shorrocks and S. Subramanian, 'Poverty: An Overview', Mimeo, UNU-WIDER, Helsinki, 2006). The following is a detailed acknowledgement of various persons and institutions for permission to use/reproduce/draw heavily on earlier published work of mine:

India International Centre and Lancer International New Delhi for the use of 'Poverty Statistics: Real Phenomena or Arithmetical Illusions? A Note', in

Malcolm S. Adiseshiah (ed.), *Mid-Year Review of the Economy 1986–87*, New Delhi: Lancer International, 1987, pp. 135–41; and 'Poverty', in Adiseshiah (ed.), *Eighth Plan Perspectives*, New Delhi: Lancer International, 1990, pp. 221–54;

Oxford University Press India, New Delhi, for the use of 'Introduction: The Measurement of Inequality and Poverty', in S. Subramanian (ed.), *Measurement of Inequality and Poverty*, New Delhi: Oxford University Press, 1997, pp. 1–53 (Readers in Economics Series) reprinted as Oxford India Paperbacks in 2000, 2002;

Oxford University Press, Clarendon, and Kaushik Basu and Ravi Kanbur for the use of 'A Practical Proposal for Simplifying the Measurement of Income Poverty', in Kaushik Basu and Ravi Kanbur (eds), *Arguments for a Better World: Essays in Honour of Amartya Sen, Volume 1: Ethics, Welfare, and Measurement*, Clarendon: Oxford University Press, 2009, pp. 435–52;

Panayotis Michaelides, Editor of the *Journal of Economic Analysis*, for the use of 'Money-metric Poverty Identification: A Cautionary Note', *Journal of Economic Analysis*, 2(1): 35–56, 2011;

The Courant Research Centre for Poverty, Equity and Growth and Stephan Klasen for the use of

'Identifying the Income-Poor: Some Controversies in India and Elsewhere', Discussion Paper 46, Poverty, Equity and Growth Discussion Papers Series, Courant Research Centre, Goettingen, Germany, 2010; and

Rammanohar Reddy and Sameeksha Trust for the use of 'Unravelling a Conceptual Muddle: India's Poverty Statistics in the Light of Basic Demand Theory', *Economic and Political Weekly*, XL(1): 57–66, 2005; '"How Many Poor in the World?": A Critique of Ravallion's Reply', *Economic and Political Weekly*, 44(5): 67–71, 2009; '"Inclusive Development" and the Quintile Income Statistic', *Economic and Political Weekly*, XLVI (4): 69–72, 2011; and 'The Poverty Line: Getting it Wrong Again', *Economic and Political Weekly*, XLVI(49): 37–42, 2011.

To Sanjay Reddy, I am most grateful for his reactions to an earlier version of this extended essay, and, much more, for sharing his views and listening to me, over many years, on the subject of this book. I am similarly indebted to D. Jayaraj, my colleague and frequent collaborator in work. A. Arivazhagan has helped with the graphics, for which my thanks to him. The editorial staff at OUP have been most supportive and conscientious in seeing this project through, and it has

Acknowledgements

been a pleasure to work with them on it. Finally, I am grateful to Nitasha Devasar for inviting me to pick up my scattered essays on the subject of this volume and to put them together in (what I hope is) a coherent and self-contained piece of work.

May 2012   S. Subramanian

1

Introduction

At the outset, I should highlight and delimit the scope of the exercise undertaken in the present essay. My concern here will be only with unidimensional—specifically, *money-metric*—poverty. In particular, I shall not be addressing any of the issues relating to the measurement of multidimensional deprivation. This is in no way to question the importance of that enterprise, but rather only to ensure clarity on what this essay will and will not deal with.

As is well-known, the measurement of income poverty (or more generally, money-metric poverty) revolves around two exercises, those of 'identification' and 'aggregation'. The identification problem is concerned with stipulating a level of income or consumption expenditure as a 'poverty line' such that those below this line are certified to be poor. The aggregation problem is concerned with combining information on the distribution of income and the poverty line with a view to coming up with a single real number that is supposed to measure the extent of poverty. Possibly the simplest real-valued measure of poverty available is the so-called 'headcount ratio', which is just the proportion of the population living below the poverty line. Insofar as the aggregation problem is concerned, the present essay's engagement in this regard will be confined to the headcount ratio.

The essay's principal concern will be with the identification of the poor in terms of a money-metric poverty threshold. The identification and aggregation exercises are, of course, crucially linked, in the straight-forward sense that what poverty line we employ will have implications for both the magnitude and trend of the measure of poverty we choose to employ. It is, indeed, precisely because of this link that the choice of poverty line is such a salient aspect of the overall poverty measurement exercise: issues of 'fact', policy, interest, and ideology are all therefore implicated in the identification exercise. One must, arising from this, expect the identification component of the poverty measurement exercise to be attended by disputation and controversy—as indeed has been the case, in India and elsewhere.

The focus in this essay will be primarily on the Indian experience and the World Bank's global poverty estimates, with some references to money-metric identification as reflected in the official United States' approach to estimating poverty. The attempt will be largely to provide a broad perspective on the facts and issues involved, without resort to any minute exploration of matters of detail. The Indian experience will be reviewed mainly in relation to official efforts at addressing the identification problem, together with a brief treatment of (especially) early engagement with the problem by academicians. The attempt will be to appraise the experience as it has obtained in the 1960s and 1970s, the 1980s, the 1990s, and thereafter. The American experience will be dealt with extremely briefly. The World Bank approach will be described, and critically appraised, with a view to elucidating a certain commonality of conceptual problems presiding over these various exercises. An attempt will be made to locate the controversies in a theoretical assessment of the appropriate space in which poverty is most sensibly assessed.

It should be noted that this essay is essentially an effort at putting together various earlier treatments of the subject by its author. It is written in the expectation that a consolidated essay on the topic might be of interest and use to a student seeking exposure to the issues involved. In the nature of things, the book draws very heavily—and often enough without benefit of quotation marks—on a number of the author's earlier works, notably Subramanian (1987, 1990, 1997, 2005, 2009a, 2009b, 2010, 2011a, 2011b, and 2011c). There are three technical addenda appended to the essay: these are meant for those with a specialized interest in these matters, and may be skipped without serious loss by the general reader.

2

Identifying the Income-Poor
Some Background Considerations

Notions and Interpretations of Poverty

As remarked earlier, it is customary to view the exercise of income poverty measurement in terms of a two-part problem: one must first *identify* the poor, and having done so, one can proceed to *aggregate* information on the distribution of incomes in order to arrive at a real number that is intended to signify the extent of poverty in the distribution under consideration. The present book is mainly about the identification issue, and accordingly, it is to this problem that we shall confine our attention. The larger concern of this extended essay is to critically assess the manner in which the identification problem has been sought to be solved in certain concrete historical settings, and the following chapters of the book are devoted to an assessment of the Indian, the US, and the World Bank experiences in this regard. However, partly as a guide to the subsequent empirical explorations just mentioned, and partly because of the background relevance of certain conceptual issues for an understanding of the complexities of the identification exercise, it is useful to undertake an independent, quick, and preliminary review of notions and interpretations of poverty. The present chapter—which draws very heavily on Shorrocks and Subramanian (2006)—is concerned with providing precisely such a broad, background overview of the subject.

To be able to tell who the poor are, it helps to be equipped with a reasonably well-defined conception of poverty, a notion of what it means to be poor. There are at least three widely-employed approaches to conceptualizing the phenomenon of poverty: the so-called *subsistence* approach, the *basic needs* approach, and the *relative deprivation* approach, all of which are described and elaborated on by Townsend (2004a, 2004b, 2004c). Under the subsistence approach, poverty is reckoned, at the individual level, in terms of deprivation with respect to fundamental physiological needs. The basic needs approach adopts a less narrow conception of needs, interpreting these to include—at the level of communities as a whole—various amenities and services. The relative deprivation approach goes even further in its assessment of human needs, by recognizing the importance not only of physiological and material wants but also of socially-dictated ones. In this interpretation of poverty, the phenomenon is seen as a shortfall from some threshold level that is determined not only by purely personal needs, considered in isolation at the individual level, but also by needs that arise from comparison with others, through the mediation of social norms of community participation and the like. This expanded notion of poverty thus also incorporates the notion of 'social exclusion'. As we move from the subsistence to the basic needs to the relative deprivation approach to conceptualizing poverty, we must expect the identification of the poor to become progressively more expansive.

How poverty is interpreted is also a function of the dimension or *space* in which it is assessed. (This is an issue to which we shall return, in some detail, in Chapter 5.) In principle, there is a plurality of spaces in which poverty can be reckoned. Amongst those that have been advanced in the literature—the reader is referred to Duclos and Araar (2005) for a lucid review— are the spaces of *utility/welfare*, *income/consumption* (or *resources*, at a more general level), and *functionings and capabilities*. No matter which space one employs, one must expect to encounter problems of a practical or a conceptual nature in its employment.

The difficulty with employing utility as a metric is that it is not directly observable, apart from the fact that it could be tricky to identify deprivation with a purely mental affect: to suggest that a mill-hand is less poor than a millionaire simply because the former feels less deprived by virtue of possessing a cheerful disposition while the latter feels more deprived by virtue of possessing a melancholic disposition is surely misleading (Sen 1985a, 1992). Additionally, there is no broad platform of agreement on the interpersonal comparability of utilities.

As a matter of practice, the space that is most widely resorted to for the assessment of poverty is that of income or consumption expenditure (the latter is generally reckoned as a more reliable indicator of welfare than the former). Comparisons of money-metric poverty can face one important problem—that of coming up with an unexceptionable price deflator in terms of which monetary values can be satisfactorily corrected for price variations across comparison regimes. This is essentially a practical problem, albeit one with signifi- cant implications for poverty comparisons across space and over time. At a more purely conceptual level, one could claim that what matters for assessing deprivation is the actual achievements of 'being and doing'—what Sen (1985a) calls 'functionings': income, one could object, is only a means, and a not necessarily reliable means, for attaining these functionings.

In terms of the objection just reviewed, to determine the poverty status of an individual the focus ought to be (illustratively) on verifying if the individual has escaped hunger, ignorance and morbidity, rather than on whether she has a high level of income, as such. This is an argument for adopting a multidimensional, as opposed to a unidimensional (money-metric), view of poverty. It should be stressed that even if one does not resort to such an argument, that is, even if one con- fines attention to a unidimensional (money-metric) view of poverty (as is done in this book), the issue of the space in which poverty is assessed continues to be a salient one. To see what is involved, consider the following. There are practitioners who would claim that the poor should be identified as those with incomes (or consumption levels) below a uniquely specified threshold. This position should be contrasted from one which asserts that there is some combination of achievements in functioning space that must be attained in order to escape poverty, and that there is no necessarily unique threshold of income (or consumption) valid for all persons and all contexts at which the specified combination of achievements in functioning space can be attained.

This last point of view has implications for yet another categorization of notions of poverty advanced in the literature—the categorization into *absolute* and *relative* concepts. The absolute/relative distinction has been seen in different lights by different practitioners, and this is no small reason for the confusion that attends the distinction. In one version of the distinction, the space in which poverty is assessed—say that of incomes—is held fixed, and an absolute conception of poverty is seen as one in which the poverty norm is a singular one, unvarying from distribution to distribution, while a relative conception is one in which the poverty norm is allowed to vary with the distribution under review, so that (for instance), the norm is permitted to increase with the general level of prosperity of the society as a whole. In a relative view of poverty of the type just described, the poverty norm may be prescribed by reference to some measure of central tendency of the income distribution: the norm, for instance, may be pitched at one-half the mean income. Sen (1983) questions the value of this sort of relativity, by pointing out that the notion more nearly captures some reckoning of *inequality* than of poverty, as such. With such a relative view of poverty, if all incomes in a distribution were to be halved, the set of identified poor persons would continue to remain the same even if some individuals, as a consequence, were to receive incomes that are inadequate to avoid starvation.

Sen (1983) advocates an alternative, more productive, way of viewing the absolute/relative distinction. In this view, the *space* in which poverty is assessed acquires crucial significance. Specifically, Sen suggests that it is sensible to interpret poverty in an absolute way in the space of functionings (as amounting, for instance, to achieving freedom from hunger, ignorance, and morbidity). Such absoluteness in the space of functionings is, however, compatible with relativities

11

or variations in the required command over income (or commodity bundles, or resources more generally). This could be the case for at least two reasons. The first—holding the *context* of comparison fixed (say within a homogeneous geographical region)—could be because of interpersonal variations in the ability to convert resources into functionings (a physically handicapped person, for instance, will typically require more resources than an able-bodied person to achieve the same absolute level of a set of specified functionings, just as, other things equal, a lactating mother will require more nutritional resources than other women in order to attain to a state of nutritional adequacy). The second reason—even assuming that all individuals have the same non-income characteristics—could arise because of *contextual* or *environmental* variations: identically constituted human beings would, for instance, require more income to avoid morbidity in an environment with poor sanitation than in one with access to clean drinking water. Hence Sen's view that it is sensible to view poverty as an absolute notion in the space of functionings, but as a relative one in the space of incomes, commodities, and resources. When the issue is viewed in these terms, it appears that the differences informing the positions of commentators such as Townsend and Sen on the absolute/relative distinction are actually more apparent than real (see Sen [1983, 1985b] and Townsend [1985] for an exchange on the subject).

The Poverty Line

Whatever underlying conception of poverty may be employed, the single most crucial practical problem confronting the poverty analyst is the specification of a *poverty line* which will separate the poor segment of a population from its non-poor segment. Two very instructive reviews of this problem are available in Ravallion (1998) and Duclos and Araar (2005), which latter has been especially useful for the present exposition. Our concern here will be with the specification of a *money-metric* poverty line, that is, a poverty line identified in monetary units as the level of income or consumption expenditure required in order to avoid poverty, which is the convention most widely employed in the unidimensional poverty identification exercise. As a matter of practical convenience, the simplest approach to adopt here would be one of comprehensive relativism, whereby the poverty line is specified as some fraction of a measure of central tendency of the distribution, such as the mean or the median or the mode. We have already seen that such relativism could do violence to a reasonable conception of poverty which, as Sen (1983) demands, must reflect some 'irreducible core' of absolutism. Two approaches that are compatible with such an absolutist orientation are the so-called 'cost of basic needs (CBN)' and the 'food energy intake (FEI)' methods. Common to both methods is the view that an essential criterion for avoiding poverty is the availability of adequate nutrition. (Greer and Thorbecke [1986] present an illuminating empirical approach to operationalizing such a view of identification and poverty assessment, while Osmani [1992] offers a comprehensive discussion of the several debates that have centred on the question of what constitutes 'adequate nutrition'.) We consider each of these methods in turn.

'Basic needs', under the CBN approach, are factored into 'food-related' needs and 'non-food-related' needs. A two-stage process is now initiated: in the first, the expenditure required to meet food-related needs is estimated; and this 'food poverty line' is employed, in the second stage, to estimate an aggregate poverty line intended to comprehend non-food needs as well. Typically, the first-stage problem is addressed in terms of the cost of a food basket that will meet some pre-specified nutritional standard (such as a calorific norm of, say, 2,400 kilocalories per person per day), while also satisfying some constraints imposed by 'palatability' considerations. One difficulty with this procedure is that there are likely to be differences in the food preferences ('palatability constraints') as between the rich and the poor. The former would typically favour more varied and expensive food baskets than the latter, and if it is the poor whose preferences must be reckoned in arriving at the 'food poverty line', then one is confronted with an awkward circularity of logic: one must first identify a 'typically poor' section of the population whose consumption pattern will serve to determine a food basket—the cost of which is supposed to guide the identification of the poor section of the population! Setting aside this problem, the second stage of the CBN approach consists in deriving an 'aggregate' poverty line from the 'food' poverty line. This can be done by dividing the food poverty line by the ratio of food expenditure to total expenditure for those whose total expenditure coincides with the food poverty line. Or, if one is inclined to be less conservative, by dividing the food poverty line by the ratio of food expenditure to total expenditure for those whose food expenditure coincides with the food poverty line. (The latter procedure will yield a typically higher aggregate poverty line because of the widely observed fact that the share of food expenditure in total expenditure declines as total expenditure increases.)

A more straightforward link between nutrition and expenditure is exploited by the FEI method, which is based on the empirical relationship—usually estimated by regression—between calorie intake and total expenditure. Once a calorie norm is specified, say 2,400 kilocalories per person per day, the corresponding level of total consumption expenditure at which the norm is achieved can be read off from the graph relating calorie consumption to total expenditure. This level of consumption expenditure is then the poverty line under the FEI method. One obvious practical advantage of employing the FEI approach to identification is that one can dispense with the need for price indices in time-series and cross-section comparisons of poverty: the poverty line is always read off directly from the intake–expenditure graph, with expenditure measured at current prices.

One shared difficulty which is a feature of both the CBN and FEI methods is that they depend crucially, for the specification of the poverty line, on the actual pattern of consumer behaviour that obtains in any given context. As we have seen, this could lead, for example, to higher urban poverty lines relative to rural poverty lines because of the relatively more diversified and expensive diets or composition of non-food commodity baskets in urban relative to rural populations. This, of course, should not be a problem if the differences in poverty lines can be traced to context-dependent differences in resources needed to achieve the same absolute functioning of, say, 'appearing in public without shame', or of 'engaging in the demands of community participation'. There could, however, be a genuine problem if the differences in the poverty lines arise on account of extravagant or idiosyncratic tastes. Disentangling causation may be hard to achieve on the ground.

It is customary to refer to the CBN and FEI methods as belonging to the class of 'objective' approaches to the identification of the poverty line. 'Subjective' approaches would typically revolve around procedures for locating the poverty line in individuals' own perceptions of what might constitute a minimum income adequate to their needs. Subjective approaches are not particularly a feature of identification procedures employed in developing countries, and we shall not deal with the issue further here, save to refer the reader interested in pursuing the matter to the work of scholars such as Groedhart, Halberstadt, Kapteyn, and van Praag (1977); Hagenaars and van Praag (1985); and Kapteyn, Kooreman, and Willemse (1988).

Complicating the Plot

Poverty, in all of the preceding discussion, has been treated as an *exact* notion: specifically, in this view, poverty status is a binary variable which allows for one of only two possible descriptions of a person, namely that s/he is poor or is non-poor. However, it is often the case that individuals are more realistically described as being more or less poor rather than as being only either poor or non-poor. This former interpretation is typically accommodated by a fuzzy view of poverty, wherein poverty status is seen as a multivalued variable: typically, the 'degree of confidence' with which a person with a given income is pronounced to be poor is postulated as some number in the continuum from zero to one, rather than as a number confined to the extremities (zero, to connote unambiguous absence of poverty, and one, to connote its unambiguous presence). Shorrocks and Subramanian (1994) is one example of the application of fuzzy logic to poverty assessment. 'Vague' predicates have also been employed in assessing multidimensional poverty, where many attributes are involved in describing the condition of deprivation: Chiappero Martinetti (1994) and Qizilbash (2003) are examples of work in this tradition.

The practice of an unambiguous categorization of a population into two mutually exclusive and exhaustive categories of the poor and the non-poor also does some violence to the notion of *vulnerability*, a subject of important recent research (see, for example, Ligon and Schechter [2003], and Calvo and Dercon [2005]). The world we live in is an uncertain one: an essentially static view of poverty, such as is a feature of a good deal of conventional analysis, does not, typically, allow for the circumstance of being pushed into poverty by the forces of various down-side risks, ranging from ill health to acts of God. Susceptibility to poverty in an unpredictably dynamic world, especially for those located just above the poverty line, is poorly captured by the specification of a poverty line that strictly separates the poor from the non-poor.

Yet another practical problem of considerable salience in assessments of poverty status has to do with the issue of *heterogeneity*. An area in which the problem of heterogeneity has found much application has to do with situations in which the income-recipient is a *household*. Households are very good examples of heterogeneous entities, that is to say, of entities whose non-income characteristics are far from being similar. In particular, households typically vary in size, and in their age and gender compositions. Specifying a household-level poverty line must then necessarily take into account these variations, in order that some appropriate sort of 'standardization' or 'equivalization' may be implemented before legitimate poverty comparisons across households can be carried out. The problem is a very general one when once we move away from the comfortable assumption of 'homogeneous populations', wherein the non-income characteristics of income-recipients are treated as being identical: the world as we know it is the very opposite of this description, and taking into account the complication of heterogeneity is an enormously difficult conceptual problem for the welfare, inequality, and poverty analyses of distributions (see Shorrocks [2004] for a comprehensive treatment of the issue).

These complications—of fuzziness, vulnerability, and heterogeneity—have been mentioned only for reasons of a small measure of completeness in the treatment of the subject. We shall not be referring to these issues again in the rest of this book. But even with the simplifying omission of these difficulties, we shall find that the problem of identification, as it has unfolded in concrete historical situations, is a vexed and difficult one: a natural habitation for differences, debates, and controversies.

3

The Poverty Line in India

The Indian Experience

The 1960s and 1970s

One of the earliest attempts at identifying a poverty line for India—see Subramanian (1997)—is contained in a paper circulated by the Perspective Planning Division (PPD) of the Union Planning Commission (1962). This document ('Perspective of Development: 1961–1976') indicates that a Working Group set up by the Government of India recommended, in July 1962, a national standard of consumption expenditure of Rs 20 per person per month at 1960–1 prices as a 'bare minimum'. To allow for price differentials between the rural and urban areas, the national standard for the latter was fixed at Rs 25 per person per month. (This, given an overall norm of Rs 20 and the rural and urban population shares, implied a rural poverty line of Rs 18.90.) The basis for these figures has never been quite clearly articulated (as was noted by Rudra [1974]), though the PPD's document does suggest that a balanced diet prescribed by the Nutrition Advisory Committee of the Indian Council of Medical Research may have played a determining role.

Indeed, the PPD document offers, in effect, a candid admission of the amount of poverty India could officially 'afford' at the time, when it observes that '... the balanced diet recommended by the Nutrition Advisory Committee together with a modest standard of consumption for other items would cost approximately Rs 35 per head. By itself, this is by no means a high standard. But at present less than 20 per cent of our people can afford it' (Planning Commission [1962], reprinted in Srinivasan and Bardhan [1974: 17]). The implication is quite clear. A poverty line of Rs 35 per person per month would have plunged 80 per cent of the Indian population into poverty: wiser counsel advocated a more modest norm of Rs 20 per person per month (which itself, however, succeeded in accommodating about 60 per cent of the population in a condition of deprivation). There is an element of déjà vu in this when we consider a finding advanced in the *Report* of the National Commission for Enterprises in the Unorganized Sector (NCEUS) 47 years after the PPD document of 1962 (Government of India [2009]). The finding is that if one were to treat Rs 20 per person per day at 2004–5 prices as a working norm for a minimum standard of living, then the proportion of the population in poverty would be 77 per cent—massively in excess of the official estimate of (roughly) 27 per cent based on the official poverty line of (roughly) Rs 12 per person per day at 2004–5 prices.

Figures such as the ones reported earlier confirm that one's estimates of poverty— and, therefore, the urgency with which one views the poverty problem and the programmes and policies one would advocate for its redress on the basis of one's perception—are seriously dependent on how one chooses to solve the identification problem. It is no surprise then that the early 1970s constituted a period of intense controversy amongst academic practitioners, on the subject of an acceptable minimum standard of living in terms of a money-metric. The interested reader is referred to a number of contributions to the debate of that period, including (though far from exhaustively) the work of Minhas (1970, 1971a, 1971b, 1971c), Bardhan (1970, 1971, 1973), Bhatty (1974), and Rudra (1974). It is no accident, but rather a reflection of the mood of the times, that the title of one of Minhas' papers (1971c) was 'Rural Poverty, Numbers' Games and Polemics'.

An attempt to link a money-metric poverty norm with a norm of nutritional adequacy was explicitly undertaken in the work of Dandekar and Rath (1971). Combining National Sample Survey (NSS) data on the distributions of both consumption expenditure and calorific consumption by expenditure size-classes, they determined that a nutritional norm of 2,250 kilocalories per person per day was achieved at a consumption expenditure level of Rs 14.20 per person per month in the rural areas and Rs 22.60 per person per month in the urban areas, at 1960–1 prices. One can see that the rural norm of Rs 18.90 suggested earlier by the Working Group far exceeds the Dandekar–Rath figure. To achieve slightly greater proximity with the Working Group's rural standard, Dandekar and Rath settled on a rural poverty line of Rs 15 per person per month; and they also rounded off the urban standard to Rs 22.50 per person per month.

The Dandekar–Rath norms came to acquire a certain standing in the Indian poverty literature, so that by the time Ahluwalia was estimating rural poverty in India, he was able to refer to the Rs 15 norm as having achieved '…a well-established pedigree…' (Ahluwalia 1978: 279). A similar acceptance, as we shall shortly see, came to characterize the norms advanced by a 1979 Task Force. In the context of inequality measurement, Shorrocks (2005) refers to a certain tendency amongst practitioners to hold on to particular formulations and indices for reasons which he traces to 'inertia' and 'network' effects. This would appear to be true also for poverty identification norms—one more example of how what is generally believed to have the force of 'scientific validity' is no more than a matter of a tacitly achieved consensus amongst a group of 'experts'.

The 1980s

The issue of specifying money-metric poverty norms for India was addressed again in 1979 in a Union

Planning Commission *Report of the Task Force on Projections of Minimum Needs and Effective Consumption Demand* (Planning Commission 1979), as part of a Sixth Plan (1978–83) exercise. While the major focus of the Task Force was on projecting effective consumption demand, it also laid the groundwork for an identification methodology which was to hold sway for a considerable period of time thereafter.

In identifying consumption expenditure poverty norms for India, the Task Force employed a nutritional norm of 2,435 (rounded off to 2,400) kilocalories per person per day in the rural areas, and a norm of 2,095 (rounded off to 2,100) kilocalories per person per day in the urban areas. These were average figures based on calorie allowances recommended by a Nutrition Expert Group in 1968. This Group had prescribed age-, sex-, and activity-specific allowances, and by employing the (then projected) age–sex–occupation population structure for 1982–3, the Task Force was able to come up with an 'average' requirement of calories for what one might call a 'representative' Indian, in each of the rural and urban areas of the country. These are the 2,400 kilocalories (rural) and 2,100 kilocalories (urban) nutritional norms referred to earlier.

The National Sample Survey Organization (NSSO) periodically publishes surveys on consumption expenditure (quinquennially from 1973–4 onwards). Households are ranked in terms of per capita consumption expenditure, and the distributional data are presented in grouped form: for each size-class interval of consumption expenditure, one has information on both the average level of expenditure and the proportion of the population in that size class. Indeed, within each size class, data are available on both the quantity and value of each of a number of food and non-food items of consumption. Employing appropriate conversion factors for the food items, it is possible to estimate the average value of calorific consumption within each expenditure size-class interval. Effectively, therefore, what is available to one is a distribution of both consumption expenditure and calorific consumption according to expenditure groups.

For 1973–4, the Task Force, employing the above two sets of data, resorted to inverse linear interpolation in order to determine the level of monthly consumption expenditure, on average, at which the rural and urban calorific norms of 2,400 kilocalories and 2,100 kilocalories per person per day were met. These turned out to be, respectively, Rs 49.09 for the rural areas and Rs 56.56 for the urban areas at 1973–4 prices. It was determined, on this basis, that the rural (respectively, urban) poverty line could be taken to be a consumption expenditure level of Rs 49.09 (respectively, Rs 56.56) per person per month. This is an example of an application of the food energy intake (FEI) method of poverty identification that was reviewed in Chapter 2.

A somewhat stylized exposition of what is involved in the above exercise is spelt out in what follows. The objective is to point to some difficulties that can arise even if we were to confine the scope of our criticism only to the 'internal' jurisdiction of the methodology employed. Among other things, it appears that a commonly supposed feature of this methodology is that it furnishes a lower bound on the proportion of the population in calorific deficit—a supposition that may not be well-founded. Table 3.1a furnishes some hypothetical unit data on consumption expenditure and calorific consumption for a population of ten persons. The cumulative distribution function $F(x)$ of expenditure x is plotted in Figure 3.1. One can now present the unit data in Table 3.1a in grouped form: Table 3.1b

TABLE 3.1a Hypothetical Unit Data on Consumption Expenditure and Calorie Consumption

Person	1	2	3	4	5	6	7	8	9	10
Expenditure Level (Rs x)	10	20	30	40	50	60	70	80	90	100
Calorie Consumption (kilocalories c)	1,200	1,600	1,800	2,000	2,200	2,100	2,400	2,400	2,400	2,420

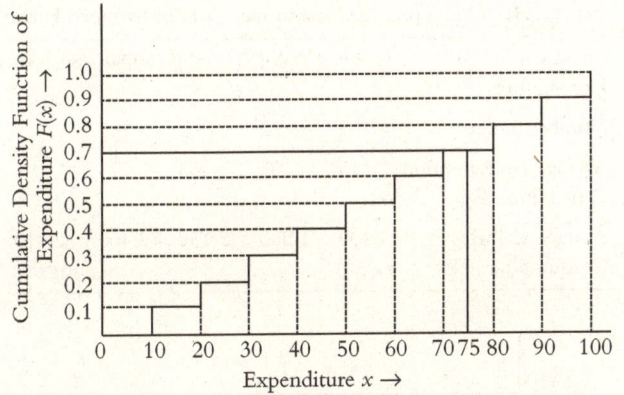

FIGURE 3.1 Distribution of Expenditure
(Plotted from Table 3.1a)

performs this task, for a particular size classification of expenditure; and in Figure 3.2, the average calorie figures (last row of Table 3.1b) are plotted against the average expenditure levels (second row of Table 3.1b), to yield the calories–expenditure graph.

If the calorific norm employed is 2,400 kilocalories, then from Figure 3.2 we can (by inverting the axes) read off the corresponding expenditure level as Rs 75. Figure 3.1 then tells us that the proportion of the population with expenditure less than Rs 75 is 70 per cent. However, notice from Table 3.1a that only (the first) six individuals have calorie consumption

TABLE 3.1b Recasting the Data in Table 3.1a in Grouped Form

Size Class of Expenditure	(0,20]	(20,40]	(40,60]	(60,80]	(80,100]
Number of Persons	2	2	2	2	2
Average Consumption Expenditure ($\bar{x}$)	15	35	55	75	95
Average Calorie Consumption ($\bar{c}$)	1,400	1,900	2,150	2,400	2,410

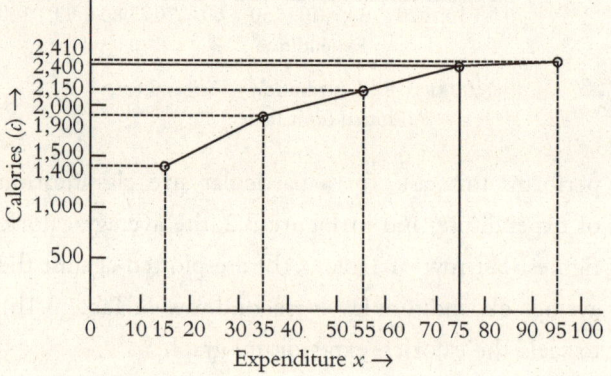

FIGURE 3.2   (Average) Calories—(Average) Expenditure Curve
(Plotted from Table 3.1b)

less than 2,400 kilocalories: the proportion in calorific deficit is only 60 per cent. That is, the method under discussion does not yield a lower bound on the headcount ratio of those under nutritional stress.

32

However, one can also easily construct an example where the headcount ratio of those in calorific deficiency exceeds the headcount ratio of those in consumption expenditure deficiency. Consider a slight alteration in the presumed calorie levels of Persons 7, 8, 9, and 10 as depicted in Table 3.1a: this yields an alternative hypothetical set of unit data on consumption expenditure and calorific intake for the ten individuals, vide Table 3.2a; and corresponding to Table 3.1b we now have Table 3.2b, which presents the unit data of Table 3.2a in grouped form. If the cutoff calorific norm is now taken to be 2,300 kilocalories, then (it can be verified from Table 3.2b that) the corresponding expenditure poverty line, derived from linear interpolation, is Rs 65. The cumulative proportion of the population with expenditure levels less than Rs 65 (see Table 3.2a) is 60 per cent, whereas the cumulative proportion of the population with a calorie intake that is less than 2,300 kilocalories is 70 per cent (Table 3.2a).

In general, a necessary condition for obtaining a match between the headcount ratios in calorific deficiency and expenditure deficiency would be the requirement of a one-to-one monotonic relationship between calorie consumption and expenditure level,

TABLE 3.2a Alternative Hypothetical Unit Data on Consumption Expenditure and Calorie Consumption

Person	1	2	3	4	5	6	7	8	9	10
Expenditure Level (Rs x)	10	20	30	40	50	60	70	80	90	100
Calorie Consumption (kilocalories c)	1,200	1,600	1,800	2,000	2,200	2,100	2,100	2,800	2,800	2,800

TABLE 3.2b Recasting the Data in Table 3.2a in Grouped Forms

Size Class of Expenditure	(0,20]	(20,40]	(40,60]	(60,80]	(80,100]
Number of Persons	2	2	2	2	2
Average Consumption Expenditure ($\bar{x}$)	15	35	55	75	95
Average Calorie Consumption ($\bar{c}$)	1,400	1,900	2,150	2,450	2,800

that is, only when, for all persons j and k, $c_j > c_k$ holds if and only if $x_j > x_k$ holds. Indeed, one would imagine that in order to obtain the headcount ratio of those in calorific deficit the straightforward procedure would be for one to directly access the cumulative distribution function of calorie consumption across individuals.

These difficulties, among others, are in fact actually acknowledged in a 1984 *Report of the Study Group on the Concepts and Estimation of Poverty Line* (Planning Commission 1984). Indeed, the Study Group reported that an application of the methodology just described to the 1977–8 NSSO consumption expenditure data revealed the following: the proportion of the rural population below the money-metric poverty line was 51.5 per cent while the proportion of the population below the nutritional norm of 2,400 kilocalories was

57.8 per cent, with the corresponding figures for the urban areas being 29.7 per cent and 49.3 per cent respectively (Table B in Planning Commission 1984). Such mismatches make it hard to give meaningful content to the notion that the money-metric poverty lines have been anchored in nutritional norms.

The Study Group examined the data on the joint distribution of the population according to both consumption expenditure and calorie consumption size-classes; a bivariate log-normal distribution fitted to these data yielded the expenditure norm corresponding to the stipulated calorific norm. Employing these expenditure norms for each of the rural and urban areas separately, the Study Group noted that the proportion of the population in expenditure deprivation was very close in magnitude to the proportion of the population in calorific deficiency. The Group's *Report* also noted that in the rural (respectively, urban) areas, four-fifths (respectively, three-fourths) of those classified as expenditure-poor were also nutritionally deprived, suggesting a relatively small misclassification of the nutritionally un-stressed as poor in relation to the expenditure norm. Arising from these findings, the Study Group recommended that the money-metric poverty lines be derived by fitting a bivariate log-normal distribution to the joint classification of the population by consumption expenditure and calorie consumption. It is not clear if this recommendation was guided by any theoretical considerations over and above the heuristic case, just discussed, in its favour.

Four other salient recommendations made by the Study Group are the following. First, the Group suggested that the nutritional norms should be changed over time to reflect the varying age–sex–occupation composition of the population; second, that the expenditure poverty line should be fixed afresh every five years on the basis of the NSSO's quinquennial data on consumption expenditure and calorific consumption (a recommendation that follows from an orthodox application of the FEI method of identification, but one that was never officially implemented and which, as we shall see later, has been championed by Utsa Patnaik [2004, 2007]); third, that the poverty lines for the years between two successive NSSO surveys be obtained by 'updating' the poverty line corresponding to the earlier survey by a suitable price index; and fourth, that a practice that had been initiated by the Planning Commission of 'adjusting' the NSSO consumption expenditure distribution be continued. The 'adjustment' in question was prompted by the observation that the mean consumption expenditure as reported by the NSS consumption surveys was lower than the mean consumption as reported by the Central Statistical Organization's (CSO) National Accounts Statistics (NAS), and that the two means were diverging over time. The Planning Commission therefore decided to scale the NSSO distribution up, uniformly, by a scale factor given by the ratio of the CSO mean to the NSS mean. The divergence between the estimates of national accounts means and income/expenditure survey means, in a number of countries, has also proved to be an issue in the estimation of country-specific and global poverty rates. It is, therefore, a problem that deserves some independent examination, as is undertaken, for the Indian context, in the following section.

Poverty Statistics and the Rules of Arithmetic

The identification problem, as we have seen, requires us to be able to classify any individual as poor or non-poor. The individual's poverty status would depend on (a) her income, and (b) the stipulated poverty line. One can see—and this observation is made in a matter-of-fact and not necessarily cynical spirit—that, in principle, poverty statistics can be manipulated by manipulating either an individual's income or the poverty line or both. Here, I will examine a particular application of this proposition to certain estimates of poverty that were put out in Volume 1 of the Seventh Five-Year Plan 1985–90 (Planning Commission 1985). (In doing so, I shall draw very heavily on Subramanian [1987 and 1990].)

According to the Seventh Plan estimates, there was a considerable decline in the proportion of the population in (money-metric) poverty between the years 1977–8 and 1983–4. The all-India headcount ratio of poverty was reported to have declined over this period, from 48.3 per cent to 37.4 per cent, this being a product of a decline in the rural ratio from 51.2 per cent to 40.4 per cent, and in the urban ratio from 38.2 per cent to 28.1 per cent. A good part of this apparent success in combating poverty was attributed to the implementation of poverty alleviation schemes such as the Integrated Rural Development Programme (IRDP), the National Rural Employment Programme

(NREP) and the Rural Landless Employment Generation Programme (RLEGP). A vigilant citizenry should be interested in knowing what is predominantly behind such claimed successes—specific programmes and policies of the state, or just the arithmetic underlying poverty statistics.

In this context, it is relevant—even if self-evident—to note that both magnitude and trend of the headcount ratio are functions of the poverty line selected, the price deflator chosen, and the distribution employed for computing the headcount ratio. In much of the academic literature of the 1970s—as in the earlier cited works of scholars such as Dandekar and Rath, Ahluwalia, and Bardhan—it was customary to employ a rural poverty line (which could be called a 'conventional' poverty line) of Rs 15 per capita per month at 1960–1 prices; to 'update' this poverty line to levels at current prices by employing the Consumer Price Index for Agricultural Labourers (CPI-AL); and to rely, for distributional information, on the NSSO data on the distribution of consumption expenditure. In all three of these matters, the Planning Commission's poverty calculations were based on differing considerations.

Specifically, the Planning Commission employed a rural poverty line of Rs 49.09 per person per month at 1973–4 prices (corresponding, as we have seen earlier, to the consumer expenditure level at which a nutritional norm of 2,400 kilocalories per person per day was observed to be realized, so this could be called a 'nutritional' poverty line). This poverty line was updated to a current prices poverty line by employing the CSO's final private consumption deflator. In the matter of the expenditure distribution employed by the Commission, the latter 'adjusted' the NSSO distribution by scaling it up uniformly by a factor given by the ratio of the CSO mean to the NSS mean, a procedure that has been referred to towards the end of the preceding section.

It turns out that whether we use the CPI-AL or the CSO price index, the nutritional poverty line is higher than the conventional one at 1960–1 prices. The implication of this for the magnitude of the headcount ratio is obvious from the following trivial proposition:

Proposition 1. Other things equal, the higher the poverty line, the larger is the headcount ratio.

It is to be noted that the CSO price index rose by a factor of 1.23 from 1973–4 to 1977–8 and by a factor of 2.07 from 1973–4 to 1983–4, while the corresponding figures for the CPI-AL price index were lower, at 1.14 and 1.84 respectively. On the other hand, the CSO index rose by a factor of 3.04 from 1960–1 to 1977–8 and by a factor of 5.11 from 1960–1 to 1983–4, while the corresponding figures for CPI-AL were higher, at 3.23 and 5.22 respectively. The implications of this for the magnitude of the headcount ratio, and how this will vary with what combination of poverty line and price deflator is chosen, are immediately apparent from the following very simple proposition:

Proposition 2. From one time period to another, the greater the proportionate increase in the price index, the larger is the magnitude of the headcount ratio in the terminal time period, other things remaining the same.

Finally, one needs to examine the consumer expenditure distribution employed by the Planning Commission for its poverty calculations. Here the observation is inescapable that the Commission tended to rely on rough-and-ready, not to say downright simplistic, assumptions. Specifically, the only available source of data on the distribution of consumption expenditure in India is the NSSO survey data (published quinquennially from 1973–4 onwards). As noted earlier, the NSS distribution's mean has in general tended to be lower than the mean reported by the CSO's National Accounts Statistics. The Commission was probably right in judging that the CSO mean is a rather better representation of the 'true' picture than the NSS mean. But to infer, as the Commission did, that a fair representation of the 'true' *distribution* is obtained by simply scaling the NSS distribution up by a factor equal to the ratio of the CSO mean to the NSS mean appears to be a dubious procedure: for note that any number of widely differing distributions are compatible with a given mean. Under the circumstances, to assume, in effect, that the NSS distribution understates each person's expenditure level by the same factor by which the NSS mean understates the CSO mean would seem to commit oneself to a drastically gross simplification, and one that surely demanded less precipitate acceptance given the seriousness of the context—that of inter-temporal poverty calculations—than was apparently forthcoming.

How poverty estimates would be affected by employing 'adjusted' expenditure distributions ('adjusted' for the difference between the NSS and the CSO means) requires a bit of working out. The exercise is aided by a consideration of certain tendencies which allow themselves to be summarized as 'stylized facts' in a way that would enable an analytical derivation of what the 'adjustment' of a distribution implies for the magnitudes and trends in the headcount ratio. Since the exercise is mildly technical, it has been relegated to an Appendix of the paper. The argument spelt out in Appendix A1 enables us to advance the following Proposition, stated here exactly as in the Appendix:

Proposition 3. Under the conditions discussed in Appendix A1, and other things remaining equal, (i) the headcount ratios corresponding to the 'adjusted' expenditure distributions will be smaller than those corresponding to the NSS distributions; and (ii) the proportionate decline over two time periods of the headcount ratio will be greater for the 'adjusted' than for the NSS distributions.

Given that there are at least two poverty lines (the conventional and the nutritional); at least two price deflators (the CPI-AL and the CSO private consumption); and at least two expenditure distributions (the NSS and the 'adjusted'), we are in a position to generate at least eight (= 2^3) variants—each variant corresponding to a particular combination of poverty line, price deflator and expenditure vector. Table 3.3 presents the headcount ratios in 1977–8 and 1983–4, and the proportionate decline in the headcount ratio over the period 1977–8 to 1983–4 for each of the eight variants.

Given Propositions 1, 2, and 3, we can see from Table 3.3 that our prior expectations are fully confirmed. First, note that for the variants in the pairs 1 and 3, 2 and 4, 5 and 7, and 6 and 8, the headcount ratio corresponding to the nutritional poverty line is always greater than that corresponding to the conventional poverty line. Next, for the variants in the pairs 1 and 2, 3 and 4, 5 and 6, and 7 and 8, only the price deflator varies. In line with Proposition 2, the headcount ratio corresponding to the CPI-AL deflator is greater than that corresponding to the CSO deflator when the *conventional* poverty line is used— and just the converse when the *nutritional* line is used. Finally, for the variants in the pairs 1 and 5, 2 and 6, 3 and 7, and 4 and 8, only the distribution employed differs. In line with Proposition 3, the headcount ratio corresponding to the adjusted distribution is always lower than that corresponding to the NSS distribution; further, the proportionate *decline* in the headcount ratio is always greater when the distribution employed is the 'adjusted' one. This last result is the one which is of immediate interest in the context of the present discussion.

The variant that appears to have been most widely used in the Indian poverty literature of the time is Variant 1. The variant employed by the Planning Commission is Variant 8. Variant 8 differs from Variant 1 in respect of all three factors—the poverty line, the price deflator and the distribution—on which the magnitude of the headcount ratio depends. The net effect on the magnitude and behaviour of the headcount ratio over time is difficult to predict *a priori*, when all three factors are allowed to vary simultaneously. But the numbers in Table 3.3 seem to suggest that Variant 8 *is* a politic choice: it reflects a sort of optimum decision in favour of the greatest decline in the headcount ratio that is compatible with absolute levels of the ratio that are not immediately and obviously unbelievable.

TABLE 3.3 Rural Poverty Profiles under Alternative Combinations of Poverty Line, Price Deflator, and Expenditure Distribution: India, 1977–8 and 1983–4

Variant No.	Poverty Line	Price Deflator	Expenditure Distribution	Headcount Ratio, 1977–8 (per cent)	Headcount Ratio, 1983–4 (per cent)	Per cent Decline in Headcount Ratio, 1977–8 to 1983–4
1	Conventional	CPI-AL	NSS	41.25	35.93	12.90
2	Conventional	CSO	NSS	36.39	34.22	5.96
3	Nutritional	CPI-AL	NSS	52.91	47.45	10.32
4	Nutritional	CSO	NSS	58.90	56.45	4.16
5	Conventional	CPI-AL	Adjusted	34.12	21.57	36.78
6	Conventional	CSO	Adjusted	29.45	20.12	31.68
7	Nutritional	CPI-AL	Adjusted	45.79	32.11	29.88
8	Nutritional	CSO	Adjusted	51.20	40.40	21.09

Source: Computations based on data in the *Report on the Second Quinquennial Survey on Consumer Expenditure, Report No. 311, 32nd Round, July 1977–June 1978*; and the *Report on the Third Quinquennial Survey on Consumer Expenditure, Report No. 319, 38th Round, July–December 1983.*

Propositions 1, 2, and 3 reveal what one may expect—from purely logical prior considerations—that poverty statistics will exhibit, without necessarily any knowledge of what is actually happening to poverty, as such. Table 3.3 shows that—depending on what combination of poverty line, price deflator and expenditure distribution we may be disposed to favour—the headcount ratio could vary from 29 per cent to 59 per cent in 1977–8, and from 20 per cent to 56 per cent in 1983–4; further, the proportionate *decline* in the headcount ratio from 1977–8 to 1983–4 could vary from 4 per cent to 37 per cent.

In the end, numbers are brutes, governed by the inflexible laws of arithmetic; and when the numbers purport to describe what is happening to poverty in our economy, it might be as well to keep at least one eye cocked on the rules of arithmetic. One should not be blamed for developing a disposition towards poverty statistics that parallels the disposition of Lord Ickenham towards the Duke of Dunstable (both characters in a P.G. Wodehouse novel): 'It is not that I don't trust you Dunstable, it is simply that I don't trust you.'

The Indian Experience: The 1990s and Early 2000s

As the preceding section will have indicated, official approaches to the measurement of money-metric poverty in India were in no very happy state as the country entered the final decade of the millennium. The official cure for the official malady was yet another official group, this time an Expert Group; and there is little to suggest that the Expert Group's recommendations did very much to improve the overall credibility of official estimates of poverty. In any event, the Expert Group did recommend at least one sensible measure, which was to discontinue the Planning Commission's highly questionable practice of 'adjusting' the NSS consumption expenditure distribution along the lines discussed in the preceding section. In the interests of brevity, the focus here will be only on a few salient and quickly summarized recommendations in the *Report of the Expert Group on Estimation of Proportion and Number of Poor* (Planning Commission 1993).

Apart from advocating a cessation of poverty calculations based on 'adjusted' distributions, the 1993 Expert Group expressed the following views:

(i) It endorsed the 1979 Task Force's methodology whereby the rural and urban poverty lines were fixed, respectively, at Rs 49.09 and Rs 56.56 per person per month at 1973–4 prices;

(ii) It suggested that 1973–4 be treated as the base year, and that the 'base year' poverty lines just mentioned be 'updated' for price changes over time (employing the CPI-AL in the rural areas and a combination of the Consumer Price Index for Industrial Workers [CPI-IW] and the Consumer Price Index for Non-Manual Employees in the urban areas);

(iii) It advised that, as a corollary, the poverty line ought *not* to be calculated by a repeated application of the Task Force procedure to each new NSSO consumption expenditure survey (which, it may be recalled, is what the 1984 Study Group had recommended), on the grounds that this approach '…allows for changes in the consumption basket…[which] would not give results comparable over time' (Planning Commission 1993: 14–15). The theme of a required invariance of the poverty line consumption basket is repeated: 'It may…be noted that any meaningful comparison, whether longitudinal or latitudinal, of incidence of poverty would require the use of same consumption basket associated with the given calorie norm' (ibid.: 16); again '... we feel that the poverty line approach anchored in a calorie norm and associated with a fixed consumption basket may be continued' (ibid.: 32); and yet again 'Having decided to accept the minimum living standard for defining poverty line normatively, we feel that it should be applied uniformly to all parts of the country for assessing poverty. The commodity basket corresponding to this norm should be standardized at the national level and applied to all States.' (ibid.: 33); and

(iv) It recommended that state-specific poverty lines be obtained by applying state-specific prices to the all-India 1973–4 poverty line commodity basket derived in accordance with the 1979 Task Force methodology.

It may be recalled that the 1984 Study Group had dwelt at some length on both (a) the divergences in the headcount ratios of the expenditure-deprived and the calorie-deprived populations, and (b) the non-overlap between the populations of the expenditure-deprived and the calorie-deprived. Some effort was also made by this Group to recommend a possible solution in terms of an expenditure poverty line to be derived from fitting a bivariate log-normal distribution to a joint classification of the population by consumption expenditure and calorie consumption. The 1993 Expert Group also takes note of these difficulties, as the following passage (Planning Commission 1993: 56) suggests:

> ... [F]or 1977–78 ... the percentages of persons below calorie norm but above poverty line were more or less the same as the percentages of persons below poverty line but above calorie norm. These percentages were between 12 and 13 for both, rural and urban areas. Due to this reason poverty ratios in 1977–78 would be more or less the same whether one adopted the calorie norm or the poverty line criterion. However, in 1983 there was a wide divergence between the percentage of those below calorie norm but above poverty line (28.29 per cent in rural areas) and the percentage of those below poverty line but above calorie norm (3.63 per cent in rural areas) ... Divergences were similar in rural and urban areas. In 1987–88, the divergence increased further (36.37 per cent and 3.97 per cent) ...

Hence, the poverty estimates based on the two criteria are widely different.

If this was a cause of serious concern regarding the soundness of the methodology recommended by the Expert Group, there is no overwhelming evidence for such concern in the form, for instance, of a *Report* saturated with misgivings or helpful suggestions addressing these problems. For a considerable period of time, the 1993 Expert Group's recommendations informed not only the official approach to estimating poverty, but also that of a number of independent scholars. In the fullness of time, and in accordance with the seasonal rites and rituals of State policy, the need for yet another Expert Group came to be Experienced. Thus was born in December 2005, by an Order of the Government of India, the next specialist team, whose *Report of the Expert Group to Review the Methodology for Estimation of Poverty* was submitted in November 2009 (Planning Commission 2009). But before dealing with the 2009 Expert Group's recommendations, there is a case for a critical appraisal of the 1993 Group's recommendations.

Official Poverty Estimates 1973–4 to 2004–5: The 1993 Expert Group's Methodology Reconsidered

The critique presented in this section is heavily dependent on Subramanian (2005). The 1993 Expert Group itself has noted, as we have seen, that the proportion of the rural population in calorie deficit classified as non-poor according to the expenditure poverty line rose significantly over time, from around 12 per cent in 1977–8 to around 28 per cent in 1983 to around 36 per cent in 1987–8. One would have expected the 'calorie drift' (a descriptive label that came to be attached to the phenomenon of a growing divergence between the inflation-adjusted expenditure poverty line and the level of expenditure at which the calorific norm was met) to occasion the Expert Group some misgiving about the apparent disconnect between the money-metric poverty line and the nutritional norm in which it was supposed to be 'anchored'. The Group, however, seems merely to have noted the problem without addressing itself to any constructive resolution of it. The problem, in some considerable measure, would appear to have eluded also the attention of independent, non-official, practitioners—but not all such.

Rohini Nayyar (1991) was one of the first commentators to note that in years subsequent to 1973–4, the stipulated calorific norms were not being met at the official poverty lines put out by the Planning Commission. Suryanarayana (1996, 2000) noted a secular deterioration in cereal consumption, especially among the poorer classes, but again no known official cognizance was taken of his observations and the implications these clearly had for the identification exercise in poverty measurement. Meenakshi and Vishwanathan (2003) have also pointed to mismatches between headcount ratios of the population in consumption expenditure deficiency and in calorific deficiency but once more the links with the validity of time-series statistics on (consumption expenditure-related) poverty were missed out. Nor has there been much evidence of a general appreciation of the relevance, for the conceptual bases of India's poverty statistics, of Townsend's (1979) views on relative poverty, or of Sen's (1983) views on absolute deprivation in the space of functionings and relative deprivation in the space of resources/

incomes (on which more in Chapter 5 of this book). Two major exceptions to the rule are provided by the papers by Panda and Rath (1999) and Mehta and Venkatraman (2000) respectively, which, in this author's view, are two of the most crucially significant contributions to the literature. Utsa Patnaik (2004, 2007) has been a consistent critic of the official identification methodology; among other writers who have adopted an adversely critical stance are Ray and Lancaster (2005), Subramanian (2005), and Reddy (2007).

Fairly elementary textbook demand theory should assist in seeing that the methodology endorsed by the Expert Group is compatible, under reasonably plausible circumstances, with a situation in which the 'calorie drift' would widen with time. The methodology has consisted in identifying the poverty line in a particular year (1973–4) with the consumption expenditure level at which a pre-specified calorific norm is actually observed to have been achieved. The calorific norm has subsequently exited the picture: what survives as 'normative' is the positive, or empirical, commodity bundle constituting the 'poverty line' level of consumption expenditure in the reference year (1973–4).

Now it is conventional to explain consumer behaviour in terms of an optimal choice of consumption bundle, given the consumer's preferences and the prices and income she is confronted with: whence the relevance, in this context, of basic consumer demand theory. Since the poverty lines in all other (non-1973–4) years are determined simply by a revaluation, at currently ruling prices, of the 'derived' poverty-line commodity bundle of 1973–4, the implicit—and in my view radically non-rationalizable—assumption underlying this methodology is that, somehow, it is only the 1973–4 pattern of consumer behaviour which is normatively relevant for the identification exercise. This last assumption, once it is brought out into the open, looks as bizarre as it is. The failure of actual calorific consumption to match the calorific norm at the official poverty lines, in the years succeeding 1973–4, can now be explained, within a simple framework of demand theory, by certain plausible patterns of over-time changes in tastes (reflecting variations in perceived needs) and prices and incomes (reflecting variations in budgetary constraints). Appendix A2 carries a mildly formal version of the argument which is dealt with non-technically in what follows here.

Consider changes in needs first. It is entirely conceivable that over time the prescribed nutritional norm fails to be met at the 'updated' money-metric poverty line simply because of a change in an individual's preference function, in terms of which she progressively desires non-food 'more urgently' than food, that is, there is a decline in the substitutability of food for non-food. It is crucial to elucidate what this sort of 'preference change' might actually connote on the ground. Specifically, it is important to guard against the notion that one 'chooses' one's 'tastes' in some unconstrained or capricious fashion. If the shape of the indifference curve is a reflection of one's scale of priorities, then it is a matter of hard sociological relevance to identify the factors that determine this scale of priorities. Here, social norms and conventions, as these evolve in response to the lifestyles of the relatively elite and affluent sections of society, and the nature of the social order that obtains, must necessarily be expected to influence the manner in which an individual effects a tradeoff among competing ends. Considerations of self-respect, itself very likely a function of the respect elicited from others, would in all probability cause a shift in 'taste' away from 'food' to 'non-food' in the context of

58

a society where feudal relations are gradually dissolving and whose better-off members are displaying considerable evidence of diversification in consumption. In such a society, contrasted with a more 'basic' earlier version of itself, there would be an irresistible compulsion for a poor person to value access to, say, at least one set of 'nice clothes' more highly in relation to food than might previously have been the case. Further, simply the fact of a greater availability of such institutions as schools and dispensaries must be expected to promote a greater relative valuation of the services provided by these institutions: the fact that school education or treatment of morbidity are now a more proximate possibility than they were must naturally lead to greater relative prioritization of books and footwear for the school child or of medicine in a time of illness. What one's needs might be, how one values them in relation to one another, and how these relativities vary across space and over time are, in short, very much a function of the dynamics of societal development rather than a product of some imagined idiosyncrasy of individual whim. There will be a return to these themes, at a subsequent stage, in the context of a discussion of some conceptual issues at the heart of the identification problem. For the moment, it may simply be noted that what are referred to as 'taste changes' are not to be interpreted as unexplainedly autonomous, or wholly 'volitional' variations in preferences among alternative commodities, but rather as phenomena which are embedded in social processes that shape perceptions regarding needs and their relative valuation.

Consider relative price changes next. If the rate of inflation in the price of calorie-intensive food is greater than the rate of inflation in the price of non-food commodities, one must expect again that the calorific norm will not be met at the 'updated' poverty line: it would no longer be optimal for the consumer to purchase the amount of food she did earlier. It could be maintained that this proposition may be true but is irrelevant for the assessment of poverty, if one subscribes to the view that what one ought to be concerned with is to specify a 'poverty line commodity bundle', and then to verify the poverty status of a person by reference to the affordability of this bundle given the prices ruling and the person's income. If the bundle is affordable, then the person is non-poor, and it is of no relevance to ask if it would be *optimal* for the person to demand this bundle. Indeed, in a seminal work on poverty measurement,

Watts (1968) is quite clear on this point: one can only provide an individual with the *means* of commanding a basket of commodities which one believes are required to avoid poverty: whether or not it is optimal for the consumer to demand this basket—so long as he has the requisite income to purchase it—cannot be a matter of relevance in determining his poverty status.

Whatever the independent merit of Watts' view, one would have to be very careful about applying a Watts-like argument to the Indian context of poverty identification under discussion. Specifically, Watts' contention appears to hold for a situation in which the exercise of identifying a 'poverty commodity bundle' is inspired by an *independent, normative* procedure for fixing standards which does not itself depend entirely on observed consumer behaviour for its determination. This condition simply does not hold for the official procedure by which the poverty line in 1973–4 was fixed. The 1973–4 poverty line was derived in terms of that level of consumer expenditure at which the specified calorific norm was observed to be realized: the determination of the poverty line for 1973–4, in other words, was crucially dependent on actual consumer behaviour; and if—as seems reasonable to believe—

consumer behaviour is actuated by a desire to do the best one can under the prevailing constraints, then it is clear that the issue of optimality can no longer be divorced from the identification exercise by reference to a Watts-like argument.

In terms of a standard and simple demand theory framework (such as the one dealt with in Appendix A2), the misapplied Watts argument which we are invited to endorse is of the following type. In Year 1 (the 'base year'), the poverty line income will be taken to be that level of income (given Year 1 prices) at which it is optimal for a consumer to demand the specified food-quantity norm; but when we arrive at Year 2, the poverty line income for this year will not be the income required, given Year 2 prices, for the food-quantity norm to be the optimal level of food consumption in Year 2, but rather the income level needed, at Year 2 prices, to command the commodity basket corresponding to the base year poverty line. This, as has been pointed out earlier, amounts to insistence on a bizarre inconsistency. In effect, we are invited to defer to the logical coherence of the notion of 'being a little pregnant': in this view, it is fine to infect the poverty line with optimality considerations in the reference year, but anathema to do so in all other years. Apparently, it is legitimate for a consumer to yield to Slutsky substitution effects in the reference year, but not in other years. Arising from this, we see a great deal of justification for the following observation made by Mehta and Venkatraman (2000: 2379): 'The definition of the poverty line, formalized by the "Task Force", contained a normative component, i.e., the calorie requirement, and an empirical component, which was the actual expenditure pattern in 1973–4. The … stand of the Expert Group has converted the empirical (behavioural) component into a norm and has made the normative component empirical.'

The budget constraint can change even when prices and monetary income remain unchanged. This could happen, for instance, because of a change in the over-time status of a commodity from that of a 'free good' to that of a 'marketized good'. Consider, for instance, the case of firewood for fuel. This is an important example of a situation in which, progressively, there has been an increasing (involuntary) reliance on the market for certain non-food commodities which were traditionally available as a part, say, of common property resources (Mehta and Venkatraman 2000). In such a situation one must expect, again, that over time the 'updated' poverty line will prove inadequate for the prescribed food-quantity norm to be an optimal choice for the consumer.

Briefly, elementary demand theory suggests (and Appendix A2 provides an analytical treatment of this issue) that there are plausible circumstances under which (a) at an income level which the official methodology equates with the poverty line, it would not be compatible with optimizing behaviour to consume food at its calorifically normative level; and (b) the level of income required to induce optimal consumption of the calorific norm will be greater than the officially stipulated poverty line. The 'calorie drift' we spoke of earlier is then, under certain circumstances, an inevitable concomitant of the official methodology.

In the official methodology, 1973–4 is the 'base' year. That is to say, 1973–4 is treated as the reference year in which the expenditure poverty line is determined as that level of consumption expenditure at which the calorific norm is observed to be realized. The poverty lines in all other years from 1973–4 onward are simply the 1973–4 line adjusted for price variations by use of an appropriate price index. Call this time-series of poverty lines the z^A series. In the foregoing discussion it has been argued that this procedure of identification is informed by a serious conceptual muddle. Such a judgment must naturally also hold for all variations on the theme of the official methodology. But if a proponent of the official methodology should still insist on allegiance to it, then it is open for one to ask, from polemical considerations, why the requirement of a unique 'poverty commodity bundle' must necessarily lead to the bundle relevant for the year 1973–4.

NSS distributional data are available quinquennially from 1973–4 onward till 2004–5 (specifically, for the years 1973–4, 1977–8, 1983, 1987–8, 1993–4, 1999–2000, and 2004–5). Why cannot the reference year be some intermediate year between 1973–4 and 2004–5, say, at random, the year 1983? In such an event, the relevant time-series of poverty lines would be given by a series z^B in which the 1983 poverty line is determined as that level of expenditure at which the nutritional norm is satisfied, and the poverty lines in all other years are obtained by correcting the 1983 poverty line for price changes by means of a price index. Analogously, one could think of a time-series z^C obtained by treating the terminal year, 2004–5, as the reference year.

The question 'why should the requirement of a unique "poverty commodity bundle" necessarily lead to the bundle relevant for 1973–4?' has sometimes provoked the response (offered in a spirit of more or less magnanimous concession) that there may be a case for treating, say, every tenth year as a reference year for the following years preceding the next reference year. The year 1973–4 would then be the reference year for the years 1973–4, 1977–8 and 1983; 1987–8 would be the reference year for the years 1987–8, 1993–4 and 1999–2000; and 2004–5 would be the reference year for 2004–5. The poverty line in 1973–4 would then be determined by the inverse linear interpolation method, and 'updated' by means of a price index for the years 1977–8 and 1983; subsequently, the poverty line for 1987–8 would again be determined by the inverse interpolation method, and updated for the years 1993–4 and 1999–2000; and so on. Call the resulting time-series of poverty lines the z^D series. Of course, the most thoroughly consistent procedure to employ would result in a time-series of poverty lines—call it the z^E series—such that the poverty line is determined in *each* year by the inverse interpolation method: this amounts, in effect, to a systematic application of the

FEI method of identification. This also, in fact, is the time-series which Patnaik (2004, 2007) demands, and is grounded in the entirely reasonable requirement that if optimality considerations are relevant in the year 1973–4, then they should be relevant in every other year. (Incidentally, this also is what the 1984 Study Group had recommended, a methodology that was subsequently explicitly rejected by the 1993 Expert Group.)

By way of illustration, one can examine the temporal profile of rural headcount ratios corresponding to each of the five temporal profiles of poverty lines just considered (z^A, z^B, z^C, z^D, and z^E) by employing data on average consumer expenditure and average calorific intake across consumer expenditure size-classes which are available from NSS compilations for three years: 1983, 1993–4, and 1999–2000 (corresponding to the NSS 38th, 50th, and 55th Rounds respectively). In what follows, the headcount ratio is computed rather crudely (via linear interpolation), and is presented as an approximation to the nearest integer. To generate the z^A profile of poverty lines, we treat 1983 as the base year and update the 1983 poverty line, by employing the CPI-AL, to obtain the poverty lines in current prices for 1993–4 and 1999–2000. The z^B series is obtained analogously, but by employing 1993–4 as the reference year, while the z^C series is generated by treating 1999–2000 as the reference year. For the z^D series, one can employ 1983 as the reference year for 1983, and switch to 1993–4 as the reference year for 1993–4 and 1999–2000. Finally, the z^E series is obtained by treating, in turn, each of the years 1983, 1993–4, and 1999–2000 as the reference year. Subramanian (2005) shows that under plausible circumstances, as one pushes the reference year forward in time one should expect to obtain larger magnitudes of the headcount ratio which will, in general, display a non-increasing trend. When the reference year is switched from time to time, one should expect to obtain a declining trend for the interval over which the reference year is the relevant one, followed by a spike when the reference year is switched. When each year is treated as a reference year, one should expect to obtain a non-decreasing trend in the headcount ratio. The actual figures for our small three-year mini time-series bear this expectation out, as one can see from Table 3.4.

For reasons that should be transparent from the magnitudes and trends of the relevant figures, the $H(z^A)$

TABLE 3.4 Poverty Profiles for Alternative Time-series of Poverty Lines: Rural India, 1983, 1993–4, 1999–2000

Year	z^A	z^B	z^C	z^D	z^E	$H(z^A)$	$H(z^B)$	$H(z^C)$	$H(z^D)$	$H(z^E)$
1983	120.03	139.93	154.39	120.03	120.03	65	75	80	65	65
1993–4	276.06	321.82	355.07	321.82	321.82	63	74	80	74	74
1999–2000	439.30	512.12	565.04	512.12	565.04	60	68	74	68	74

Source: Calculations are based on the following Reports of the National Sample Survey Organization: *Report on the Third Quinquennial Survey on Consumer Expenditure*, Report No. 319, 38th Round, July–December 1983; *Level and Pattern of Consumer Expenditure*, Report No. 402, 50th Round, July 1993–June 1994; and *Level and Pattern of Consumer Expenditure*, Report No. 457, 55th Round, July 1999–June 2000.

Note: z^A, z^B, z^C, z^D, and z^E refer to the five alternative poverty lines referred to in the text, and measured in rupees per person per month; and $H(.)$ refers to the headcount ratio, measured in per cent terms, corresponding to each poverty line.

numbers, namely the headcount ratios corresponding to the z^A profile of poverty lines (which reflect the official methodology) are the most optimistic ones available for projection, while the $H(z^E)$ numbers (which reflect a *non-declining* trend) could legitimately be regarded, by any Government facing re-election, to be a fate worse than death. The $H(z^B)$ and $H(z^D)$ profiles, while displaying non-increasing trends like the $H(z^A)$ numbers, also betray uncomfortably large magnitudes; and the $H(z^D)$ numbers display a mixed up-and-down story. Table 3.4 is a good example of the sort of outcome the poet William Empson warned against when he said: 'You don't want madhouse and the whole thing there.'

It could be maintained, of course, as has sometimes been done in response to criticism, that all that the official statistics convey is an 'if–then' proposition: *if* the poverty line series is the z^A series, *then* $H(z^A)$ is the resulting poverty profile. How far does this go? Exactly as far as the following if–then proposition does: *if* the poverty line series is the z^E series, *then* $H(z^E)$ is the resulting poverty profile. The problem is that these sorts of statements convey little in the absence of any hard engagement with the plausibility of the antecedent.

The real difficulty arises from the recognition that if it is fine to employ the z^A series, then there can be no compellingly logical grounds for rejecting any of the z^B, z^C, z^D, or z^E series; *per contra*, if there is anything objectionable in any of the z^B, z^C, z^D, or z^E series, then a similar stricture should apply to the z^A series as well.

And there the matter must rest, as we turn now to a very brief consideration of the prescriptions of the newest (2009) Expert Group.

Identification According to the 2009 Expert Group

The present discussion of the 2009 Expert Group's recommendations, contained in the *Report of the Expert Group to Review the Methodology for Estimation of Poverty* (Planning Commission 2009) will be based considerably on Subramanian (2011c). Also, the critique will be confined to the *identification* aspect of the methodology. That is, the innovations relating to price indices employed to express the poverty lines at 'constant prices', both across space and over time, will not be taken up for discussion. Similarly, I will not discuss here the recommendations made in respect of the appropriate recall period to be selected in employing the NSSO's consumption expenditure estimates. These issues, properly speaking, do not fall within the purview of the basic principles that (should) govern the specification of a money-metric poverty line.

If one takes the identification issue to constitute the heart of the problem of conceptualizing money-metric poverty, then it is hard to escape the conclusion that the 2009 Expert Group's recommendation in this regard is quite disappointing. This is the more so when one considers the principal motivation for the Group's work, as has been set out in the *Report* itself (Planning Commission 2009: 1): 'There has been a growing concern on the official estimates of poverty released by the Planning Commission. The official poverty estimates have been severely criticized on various counts. In view of this, the Planning Commission set up an expert group ... to examine the issue and suggest a new poverty line and estimates.' To continue with the 1993 Expert Group's poverty lines would have been a plainly unsustainable prescription, so it is not surprising that the 2009 Group advocates a different set of rural and urban poverty lines. What, however, is regrettable is the failure—as I see it—of the new Group to come up with an alternative methodology that lends itself to cogent, convincing, and logically argued justification. It is difficult not to see this exercise as a wasted opportunity.

It is noteworthy that the 2009 Expert Group, like its 1993 predecessor, perceives comparability of poverty estimates across space and over time as residing in the requirement of an invariant 'poverty line' commodity bundle. The new Group parts company from the old one in the matter of the precise commodity bundle that is to be treated as invariant across poverty comparisons. In the 2009 exercise, the commodity bundle identified is the one pertaining to the year 2004–5, the latest year (at the time) for which the NSSO's quinquennial consumption expenditure survey (61st Round) was available. The bundle is identified as the one corresponding to a consumption expenditure level, in urban India, of Rs 578.8 per person per month at current (2004–5) prices. This consumption expenditure level, in turn, simply happens to be the 2004–5 urban poverty line that would be dictated by the 1993 Expert Group's methodology—it is the 'updated' version of the per capita monthly expenditure level, for urban India, at which the urban nutritional norm of 2,100 kilocalories per person per day was realized in 1973–4. It is therefore puzzling to find the following observation in the *Report* (Planning Commission 2009: 7–8): '…a conscious decision was taken by the Expert Group to move away from anchoring the PL [poverty line] in [a] calorie norm as in the past…'. One can only interpret this to mean that while the urban poverty line of Rs 578.8 per person per month which the Expert Group plumped for happens to be the updated value of the observed expenditure level in 1973–4 corresponding to the nutritional norm of 2,100 kilocalories per person per day, this fact in itself apparently had nothing to do with the Group's choice; but then what fact did actually dictate the Group's choice remains something of a mystery.

The choice in question is sought to be explained in the Expert Group's *Report* (Planning Commission 2009: 1) in terms, *inter alia*, of '…an inescapable element of arbitrariness in specifying the numerical nominal level of [the] PLB [Poverty Line Basket]', and of what might be dictated '…in the interest of continuity…'. Indeed, there is some considerable vagueness in the rationalization resorted to, and one suspects the reason for this resides in some divergence between the Expert Group's theory and its practice. In theory, the Group has apparently been guided by the belief that it is some normative commodity basket that ought to yield the poverty line, whereas in practice it is actually a predetermined poverty line that has been employed to generate the commodity basket in question. This confusion is suggested by the cumbersome semantics of the *Report*'s assertion that '[u]nderlying [the] consumption poverty line is the reference poverty line basket (PLB) of household goods and services consumed by those households at the borderline separating the poor from the non-poor' (ibid.: 1). A simpler expression for the phrase 'borderline separating the poor from the non-poor' is, presumably, that old-fashioned term 'poverty line'. It follows then that the just-cited assertion in the *Report* can be rephrased to read: 'Underlying the consumption poverty line is the reference poverty line basket … consumed by those households at the poverty line.' This approach seems to require that we need a normative commodity bundle to determine the poverty line in order to determine the normative commodity bundle to…

Such circularities were surely avoidable. If they have not, in fact, been avoided, it is perhaps because of the Expert Group's anxiety to specify some poverty line that could be judged to be plausible from some independent (unspecified) considerations, and *then* come up with an empirically corresponding commodity bundle, one that would be invariant across space and over time, and would allow for its context-specific valuation at context-specific prices as a means of generating context-specific poverty lines. This stratagem, in turn, may well have been dictated by the anxiety to advance an estimate of poverty which escapes both the charge of being unrealistically low and the sin of being demoralizingly high. The objective, presumably, was to discover the virtue of a golden mean between the somewhat credulity-straining niggardliness of the official (1993 Expert Group) poverty line and the disturbingly anarchic generosity of the Rs 20 per person per day poverty line of the National Commission for Enterprises in the Unorganized Sector. The most pressing rationale for the method adopted by the 2009 Expert Group appears to have been, ironically, a desire to avoid controversy.

At the official Planning Commission poverty lines endorsed by the 1993 Expert Group, the rural head-count ratio in 2004–5 was 28.3 per cent, while the corresponding urban headcount ratio was 25.7 per cent. As the *Report* of the 2009 Expert Group puts it (Planning Commission 2009: 1): '… [the urban headcount ratio] is generally accepted as being less controversial than its rural counterpart at 28.3 per cent… [which] has been heavily criticized as being too low.' Again, on p. 6 of the *Report* (ibid.: 6), we have:

> … the latest available official estimate of rural poverty ratio of 28.3 per cent for 2004–05 is widely perceived to be too low … while the corresponding urban proportion of 25.7 per cent … is less controversial in terms of the broad order of magnitude of extent of urban poverty. [Arising from this,] … the PLB [Poverty Line Basket] was taken to be [the] MRP [Mixed Recall Period] equivalent of [the] PCTE [per capita total expenditure] corresponding to 25.7 per cent of the urban BPL [below poverty line] population … As urban living standard is generally regarded as better than and preferable to its rural counterpart, the Expert Group recommends that the purchasing power represented by the MRP-equivalent PCTE underlying [the] all-

India urban HCR [headcount ratio] of 25.7 per cent be taken as the new reference PLB for measuring poverty and made available to both the rural and the urban population in all the states after correcting for urban–rural price differentials as well as urban and rural state-relative-to-all-India price differentials.

Briefly, the commodity composition of the urban poverty line of Rs 578.8 in 2004–5 (the so-called poverty line basket [or PLB]) is revalued at rural prices to yield a corresponding rural poverty line (which turns out to be Rs 446.7 per person per month at 2004–5 prices); similarly, the PLB is valued at state-level rural and urban prices respectively, to yield state-level rural and urban poverty lines for 2004–5, which is the new reference year. Inter-temporally, poverty lines in any year are to be derived by revaluing the 2004–5 PLB at current prices. This brings us back to a point made earlier: while the *Report* is careful to distance itself from the charge of anchoring its poverty line in a calorie norm, one wishes it had been equally careful to amplify on the issue of what its poverty line actually *is* anchored in. As far as one can tell, the choice of poverty line has been predominantly determined by a view of what constitutes a plausible headcount ratio. This is a very hard act to follow for those of us who have been brought up to believe that one infers the headcount ratio from a normative poverty line, and not the poverty line from the less unacceptable of two headcount ratios, which are distinguished only by the fact that they happen to be the latest available estimates thrown up by an earlier faulty methodology.

Indeed, under the latter approach, one might choose as the reference year *any* year—for example 1993–4—in which the official estimate of the urban headcount ratio (32.6 per cent) was more 'plausible' than that of the rural headcount ratio (37.2 per cent). The problems associated with choice of the reference year are here exactly the same as those attending the 1993 Expert Group's approach. Thus, it is not immediately clear why it is a virtue that the 'poverty line basket' '…incorporates the latest available data on observed pattern of consumer behaviour in 2004–5' (Planning Commission 2009: 7): this may afford some comfort if we are comparing 2004–5 poverty estimates with 2009–10 poverty estimates, but by the same token, there may be a case for employing 1993–4 as the reference year if we are comparing 1987–8 poverty estimates with those for 1993–4. Yet another case that has been advanced in favour of the new poverty line (ibid.: 8) is that '... the revised minimum calorie norm for India recommended by FAO is currently around 1800 calories per capita per day which is very close to the average calorie intake of those near the new poverty lines in urban areas (1776 calories per capita) and higher than the revised FAO norm (1999 calories per capita) in rural areas in the 61st round of NSS.' But surely, this is a purely fortuitous outcome, and one fails to see the significance of these sorts of circumstantial detail. On the other hand, if the choice of the poverty line had indeed been influenced by congruence with a nutritional norm, then we would be back in the world of the 1993 Expert Group! Also, apparently counting in favour of the 2009 Group's choice of poverty line is that it '... happens to be close to, but less than, the 2005 PPP $1.25 per day poverty norm used by the World Bank in its latest world poverty estimates' (ibid.). Whether or not this is good advertisement for the poverty line is at least debatable: it must be noted that the World Bank's global poverty estimates are by no means widely perceived as being acceptable, and are, indeed, severely discredited in certain quarters (the reader is referred to the particularly important work, in this context, of Reddy and Pogge [2010]).

The 2009 Expert Group is also of the view that 'external validation checks' carried out by it suggest that the actual expenditures incurred on nutritional, educational, and health outcomes at the prescribed poverty line expenditure levels in 2004–5 are adequate to cover normative levels stipulated by the Group in this regard. In the matter of normative food expenditure, the Expert Group specifies this level by reading off the level of food expenditure, from the cumulative density function of expenditure on food, corresponding to the proportion of the population under nutritional stress (interpreted as the simple average, obtained from National Family Health Survey-III data for 2005–6, of the headcount ratio of under-five underweight children, the headcount ratio of women in the age group 15–49 with low body mass index, and the headcount ratio of men in the age group 15–49 with low body mass index). Assuming, for a moment, some merit to this method of estimating the normative food expenditure level, at least one difficulty with such a 'validation check' is represented in Figure 3.3. In Figure 3.3 we have three (hypothetical) cumulative density functions (cdfs) for food expenditure, where expenditure is represented in 'real', that is, 'constant prices' terms. The cdf labeled 1 refers to the reference year, the cdf labeled 0 refers to a year preceding the reference year, and the cdf labeled 2 refers to a year succeeding the reference year. Suppose H_1 is the headcount ratio of those under nutritional stress in the reference year. From cdf 1 we can see that the expenditure level corresponding to the headcount ratio H_1 is X_1^*. Effectively, the Expert Group employs X_1^* as the normative level of adequacy for food expenditure. Suppose also that X_1^* is the observed level of expenditure on food at the poverty line in each of the Years 0, 1, and 2. Additionally, suppose that H_0 and H_2 are the proportions of the nutritionally deprived populations in Years 0 and 2 respectively. Then Figure 3.3 suggests that the normative levels of food expenditure in Years 0 and 2 should be, respectively, X_0^* ($> X_1^*$) and X_2^* ($> X_1^*$). The actual food expenditure is adequate to cover the normative requirement in Year 1, but not in Years 0 and 2. How, in other words, can we tell *a priori* that just because the poverty line expenditure on food is adequate for a certain 'normative' food expenditure level in the reference year, this will also hold for all other years?

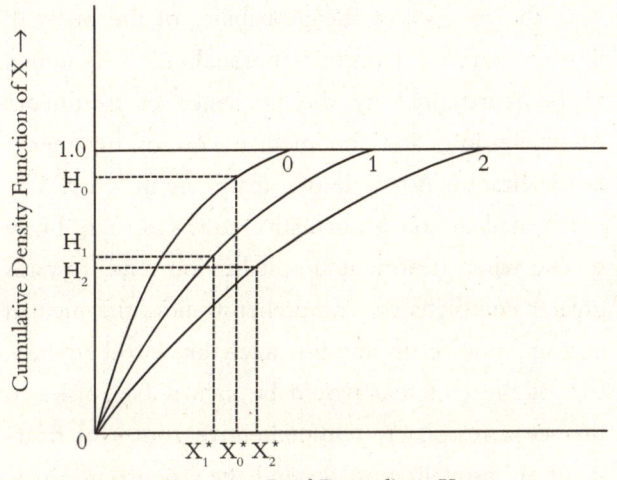

FIGURE 3.3 Determining Normative Food
Expenditure Levels

The normative level of expenditure on education
is taken to be given '…by the expenditure required
at state-specific median cost (derived from the 61st
round employment–unemployment survey) for send-
ing *all* school-going (in 5–15 years' age group) children
in the household at the PCTE to school…' (Planning
Commission 2009: 9). The normative level of expenditure on health is taken to be given by the expected
value of expenditure on treatment/hospitalization,

itself the product of the probability of the onset of illness requiring treatment/hospitalization (assumed to be represented by the incidence of treatment/hospitalization) and the median cost of treatment/hospitalization. A couple of remarks are in order. Why is the median cost a normative cost? Costs are likely to rise when treatment/hospitalization tends towards greater completeness/comprehensiveness: the median cost in a poor economy is scarcely likely to be reflective of the cost that would be incurred in order to finance a reasonably comprehensive course of treatment or hospitalization. Second, the proportional incidence of treatment/hospitalization is unlikely to be the probability of the onset of illness *requiring* treatment/hospitalization: the true incidence of illness requiring treatment will, in an environment of poor affordability, typically be larger than the incidence of illness actually treated. There is therefore good reason to believe that these 'normative' expenditure levels on education and health are underestimates.

Indeed, a simple back-of-the-envelope exercise should provide a rather more robust 'external validation' (or failure of validation) than is afforded by the convoluted tests proposed by the Expert Group. The

Expert Group's urban poverty line for Tamil Nadu in 2004–5 is reported to be nearly Rs 560 per person per month, or (without allowing for economies of scale), Rs 2,240 for a household of four members per month. To suggest that such a household would not, in 2004–5, have been in poverty strikes the present author (as a resident of Tamil Nadu's capital city) as being optimistic in a grimly determined way. In 2004–5, a modest tea-shop single-dish meal (such as a plate of lemon rice) would have cost Rs 10. Allowing two meals a day to keep out hunger, a household of four would require Rs 80 per day to spend on food. Let us cut this requirement down to Rs 60 per day to take (exaggeratedly unreal) account of the fact that home-cooked food is cheaper. This works out to Rs 1,800 per month (30 days). A modest (by which one means cramped and depressing) one-room house with attached kitchen and common toilet (for a family of four) would have easily commanded a monthly rental of Rs 1,500 in Chennai in 2004–5. Adding this to the food expenditure requirement of Rs 1,800 already brings up the total to Rs 3,300—making for a deficit, in relation to the poverty line of Rs 2,240, of Rs 1,060. And we have not even counted the cost of education or clothing or transport or the occasional movie or cigarette, not to mention such exotica as a broken bone or a bout of typhoid. This does mark a contrast from the situation as projected by the *Report* of the Expert Group (Planning Commission 2009: 2) when it says:

> Even while moving away from the calorie norms, the proposed poverty lines have been validated by check-ing the adequacy of actual private expenditure per capita near the poverty lines on food, education and health by comparing them with normative expen-ditures consistent with nutritional, educational and health outcomes. Actual private expenditures reported by households near the new poverty lines on these items were found to be adequate at the all-India level in both the rural and the urban areas and for most of the states.

One is irresistibly reminded here of the fate of G.V. Desani's (1948) immortal comic hero H. Hatterr when he recalls the head of his orphanage school from the days of his childhood:

> The sort of loco parentis who'd shower on you a penny, and warn you not to squander it on woman, *and* wine, *and* song!

4

Poverty Thresholds Elsewhere
The US and the World Bank Approaches

The US Experience: A Brief Description

The first section of this chapter—which draws heavily on Subramanian (2010)—will deal briefly with the general methodology informing the official statistics on poverty put out by the United States Federal Government, and the rest of it will be given over to an assessment of the World Bank's estimates of global poverty. The approach to identifying poverty thresholds for the US is closely associated with the efforts, in this regard, of Mollie Orshansky (see, among other works of this author, Orshansky [1965]). A highly instructive account of the evolution of these poverty norms is available in Gordon Fisher (1992), and his paper is strongly recommended as required reading for the interested researcher. In the present short summary (which is entirely dependent on Fisher's account), the emphasis will be only on certain essential aspects of the conceptual and logical bases of the identification approach adopted in the official US methodology.

In particular, all matters of detail relating to the distinction between farm and nonfarm households, and to variations in the size and age–gender composition of households, which were of crucial empirical import for the development of the US poverty thresholds, will here be ignored. To keep the focus restricted to what is of conceptual interest in the identification problem, it is useful to proceed 'as if' there were only one type of household in society, with a unique size and age–sex profile. Orshansky's early effort at identifying a poverty line for such a representative household in 1963 can be summarized in terms of the following steps.

First, the Agriculture Department of the US Government had advanced four alternative 'food plans' of varying orders of 'liberalism', of which the two most stringent ones (in declining order of stringency) were the so-called 'low cost' and 'economy' plans. These were the food baskets which Orshansky employed to construct her poverty thresholds. For our purposes, let us simplify matters by supposing that there was just one such food plan to reckon with. This food plan can be seen to have been derived from the food consumption patterns of the population constituting the poorest third of the income distribution, data on which were available in a Household Food Consumption Survey conducted by the Agriculture Department in 1955. The cost of the food plan at 1963 prices yielded the 'food' component of a possible 1963 poverty line that could be constructed.

The next step in the construction of the poverty line resided in employing the food component of a minimum standard of living in order to determine the overall minimum standard. To achieve this end, Orshansky resorted to an application of 'Engel's Law', which is the proposition that, beyond a point, the share of income spent on food declines as income increases. According to the Household Food Consumption Survey (1955), for the economy as a whole, the average proportion of income spent on food was one-third. Employing this as a norm, Orshansky reasoned that a household must have an income at least three times the cost of the food plan in order to be able to just afford it.

This level of household income, then, could serve as a poverty threshold. This is an example of an application of the 'Cost of Basic Needs' method of identification discussed in Chapter 2.

Having thus arrived at a poverty line for 1963, the next step was to determine how it should vary over time. In 1969, it was decided that the Federal Government's official statistics on poverty would be based on the 1963 poverty threshold (determined in accordance with the procedure spelt out in the preceding paragraph) and corrected, for price changes in subsequent years, by employing the US consumer price index (CPI). In 1973, an official subcommittee on updating the poverty threshold recommended that the food plan be revised, to take account of contemporary patterns of food consumption, every once in ten years; and that (apart from correcting for price changes) the poverty line be changed once in ten years by multiplying the cost of the (revised) food plan by the reciprocal of the currently obtaining ratio of income spent on food to total income (a quantity that can be conveniently summarized in the term 'multiplier'). A further recommendation was that at the end of every decade, the poverty estimates of the preceding ten years be recalculated employing current-prices poverty lines corresponding to the poverty line relevant for the first year of the new decade.

As it happens, the multiplier was never really changed from its initial value of 3. Nevertheless, it is interesting to ask what the implications would be of an inter-temporally varying multiplier, such as was recommended by the 1973 subcommittee on updating the poverty threshold. As in the context of India's poverty statistics, an issue of crucial interest in the case of US poverty statistics relates to the inter-temporal comparability of poverty estimates. To see what, in essence, is involved, let us assume that a new Consumption Expenditure Survey can be carried out every year, so that data are available annually on both the food consumption patterns of the poorest third in the income distribution and on the economy-wide ratio of income spent on food to total income. In principle, that is, the poverty line is assumed to be amenable to 'updating' every year, through an annual revision of both the food plan and the multiplier. Would such a continuously, annually 'updated' time-series of poverty lines make for an inter-temporally comparable set of poverty estimates?

Of relevance here is Amartya Sen's (1983) proposition that there is an absolute core to poverty, a notion which tends to be denied by allowing the poverty standard to vary with particular features of the income distribution one happens to be confronted with. The 'relativity' involved in the 'updating' procedure described in the preceding paragraph can be understood in terms of a simple numerical illustration. Imagine two points in time, labelled Year 1 and Year 2 respectively. Suppose that, for the economy as a whole, X_t is the aggregate expenditure on food and Y_t is the aggregate income in Year t ($t = 1, 2$). Assume there is no variation in the price level over the two years under review. Assume further that $X_1/Y_1 = 1/3$ (so the multiplier in Year 1 is 3), and that every person's income, in Year 2, declines to exactly one-half of her income level in Year 1. It is plausible, though, that the level of expenditure on food, which can be sticky downward, continues to remain at X_1 in Year 2. Let us also assume that the food plan remains unchanged, and that its cost remains the same, at F, in both Years 1 and 2. Then, one can see that the poverty line in Year 1, PL_1, is $3F$. The multiplier in Year 2 is Y_2/X_2; since $Y_2 = Y_1/2$ and $X_2 = X_1$ by assumption, the multiplier in Year 2 is $(1/2)(Y_1/X_1)$, or

3/2, since, as we have seen, $Y_1/X_1 = 3$. The poverty line in Year 2, PL_2, is then $1.5F$. In Year 2, every person's income is just one-half of their income in Year 1, but since the poverty line has also halved from $3F$ to $1.5F$, one must conclude that the set of identified poor persons in Year 2 is exactly the same as the set of identified poor persons in Year 1. This judgment, which is scarcely persuasive, is an outcome of the 'relative' element that resides in the poverty identification procedure.

The alternative to this is to preserve invariance of the poverty line in 'real income space', that is, to allow for inter-temporal variations in the (nominal) poverty lines only for reasons of inter-temporal variations in the price level. This immediately presents us with a problem which we have encountered earlier in the context of India's poverty statistics (Chapter 3 of this book). The problem is this: given a K-year time horizon, is there any non-arbitrary reason for privileging any one particular year as the 'reference year' over the other years? That is, are the food plan and multiplier of any one particular year more normatively plausible than the food plan and multiplier of any other year? The question is also of serious practical import, because one must expect the magnitude, and indeed the trend, of poverty estimates to be a variable function of which year one chooses to treat as the reference year; and, in the end, it would be hard to justify the validity of some one particular profile of poverty estimates in relation to other equally logically compelling (or un-compelling) profiles.

In sum, it would appear, from this brief consideration of the US experience, that logical difficulties in the conceptualization of money-metric poverty are not a feature only of India's official statistics on deprivation. This is confirmed even more strongly when one considers the World Bank's approach to estimating global poverty.

The World Bank's Estimates: Background

This and the following sections lean heavily on the *Economic and Political Weekly* (*EPW*) (2008) and Subramanian (2009a). The discussion follows the pattern of *EPW* (2008), which was an editorial on the World Bank's latest poverty estimates, and Subramanian (2009a), which was a response to a reply by Martin

Ravallion (2008) to the *EPW* editorial. To set the discussion going, it is useful to quote at some length (but with a few minor deviations) from the editorial in question (2008: 5, 6):

> What is it that is actually available to the interested consumer of statistics on global poverty? Given constraints of space, it would be excusable to confine oneself to two salient sets of work in this area. First, we have a sequence of poverty estimates put out by the World Bank that have been prepared by its staff. Second, we have a sequence of critiques of the World Bank's work that have led to responses and counter-responses. In 2008 the Bank came out with new and revised estimates of national and global poverty, estimates that attracted a considerable amount of attention. The organization has so far come up with three sets of global poverty estimates, all of these being headcount ratios of the population living below poverty lines specified in the money metric. The first, carried in the Bank's *World Development Report (WDR) 1990*, employed a poverty line of $1 (actually $1.02) per day at 1985 purchasing power parity (PPP), on the basis that the domestic poverty lines of eight of the poorest countries in the world clustered around this figure. The second, carried in the 2000–01 *WDR*,

employed a poverty line of $1.08 per day at 1993 PPP, which was the median of the poverty lines of the ten poorest countries. The third set of estimates, released in a World Bank working paper, employs a poverty line of $1.25 per day at 2005 PPP, this—in yet another innovative justification—being the average of the national poverty lines (in terms of consumption per capita) of the poorest fifteen countries of the world. (For discussions of the relevant methodologies underlying the three sets of estimates, the reader is referred, respectively, to Ravallion, Datt, and van de Walle 1991, Chen and Ravallion 2000, and Chen and Ravallion 2008.)

As may be expected, levels, trends, and regional distributions of poverty are all variable functions of the particular poverty line employed. Since justification has been claimed for each poverty line at the time of its broadcast, this makes it hard to repose much confidence in these exercises. The latest estimates—apparently provoked by the availability of new (2005) information on PPP exchange rates due to the efforts of the International Comparison Programme (ICP)—suggest that the levels of the headcount ratios reported in earlier studies by the Bank are lower than warranted, primarily because the price level in China, until now a largely unknown quantity, had previously been underestimated. If the bad news is on the front of levels, the good news, we are told, is on the front of trends. The elaborate title of the working paper carrying the latest estimates says it all: 'The Developing World Is Poorer Than We Thought, But No Less Successful In The Fight Against Poverty.'

How credible is all this as a description of what has been happening to global poverty? Sanjay Reddy (an economist) and Thomas Pogge (a philosopher), among others, have had a number of compelling criticisms to offer which, in my view, have been inadequately addressed by the World Bank's researchers (see, for example, Pogge and Reddy 2006, Reddy and Pogge 2010, and Ravallion 2010).

These issues—in terms of the adequacy of the poverty lines, and the problems they pose for comparability across space and over time—are taken up for more detailed examination in the sections that follow.

On the Lowness of the International Poverty Lines

First, as EPW (2008) suggests, 'dollar a day' (or thereabouts) poverty lines may well be little more than 'destitution lines'. It is sometimes pointed out (see, for example, Ravallion 2008) that the World Bank's international poverty line (IPL) is based on the national poverty lines of a set of the poorest countries of the world. Let us set aside the fact that at different points of time there have been differences in the numbers and composition of these poorest countries, as also in the basis of the relationship between the IPL and country-specific poverty lines. At a more basic level, it is not clear why it is the poorest countries' poverty standards that must serve as the poverty standard for the world as a whole. There are two kinds of classificatory errors one can make, call these Type I and Type II errors respectively (see also, in this connection, Cornia and Stewart [1995]). A Type I error is one in which a person is wrongly counted as non-poor, and a Type II error is one in which a person is wrongly counted as poor. One would imagine that a Type I error is the graver sort of mistake to commit. In a matter as serious as identifying a person's poverty status, if one must make a mistake, then it would appear to be doing less harm if one were to err (within limits, of course) on the side of generosity than on the side of niggardliness. Thus, if z_i is the national poverty line of the ith of

n countries constituting the world, then a procedure aimed at avoiding a Type I error would pitch the IPL at the level $\bar{z}$, where $\bar{z} \equiv max_i \{z_i\}$, that is, $\bar{z}$ is the highest of the n countries' national poverty lines (and is likely to be the poverty norm of the richest of the world's nations). The Bank's procedure, on the other hand, seems to be geared to avoiding a Type II error, and is close in spirit to pitching the IPL at the level $\underline{z}$, where $\underline{z} \equiv min_i \{z_i\}$, that is, $\underline{z}$ is the lowest of the n countries' national poverty lines (and is likely to be the poverty norm of the poorest of the world's nations). Even a procedure which avoids both extremes would endorse an IPL higher than \$1.25 per person per day at 2005 PPP: by Ravallion's (2008) own estimation, the average of all except the poorest countries (from, presumably, a compilation of seventy-five national poverty lines) is twice as high, at \$2.50.

The average official poverty line in the US, Ravallion (2008) tells us, is \$13 a day. The World Bank's prescribed IPL of \$1.25 a day *is less than 10 per cent of the US poverty line*. I imagine an American living in, say, California, on \$1.25 a day at 2005 PPP is entitled to feel s/he is living in circumstances of destitution. It seems unlikely that the World Bank would be disposed to correct the perception of such a hypothetical Californian by counselling calm reasonableness to her/him. It is then fair to entertain the expectation that the Bank should adopt the same stance towards a very real Sierra Leonean or Bangladeshi or Ecuadoran living on $1.25 a day at 2005 PPP. After all, the World Bank is supposed to be a *world* bank. It is easy enough to dismiss this as virtuous counsel on a matter of manners. It is, however, fundamentally a matter of logic that is involved as should be apparent if we were to take seriously what Ravallion (2004: 15) himself has said of the rationale underlying the Bank's IPL: 'For our global poverty counts, we have but one overriding concern—that two people with the same standard of living, measured by their command over commodities, be treated the same way no matter where they live.' In light of this, Ravallion's (2008: 78) observation tends somewhat to lose its rhetorical edge when he asks: '… India's official poverty line is about $1.00 a day using the same PPPs … So if $1.25 marks "destitution" what are we to make of India's national poverty line?'

It is instructive also to dwell for a moment on a particular construction of the dollar-a-day IPL due to Ravallion (2010: 88): 'The "$1 a day" line aims to judge poverty in the world as a whole by the standards of what poverty means in poor countries'. This sentiment suggests that what poverty does, or should, mean in poor countries is credibly reflected in the national poverty lines of these countries. It is not self-evidently obvious that such is indeed the case, nor—if this is an intended interpretation—that the national poverty lines of poor countries invariably reflect perceptions of poverty that are a product of democratic consultation or informed public reasoning. (Such an interpretation certainly seems to be stretching it a bit when the poverty lines in question have been prescribed by the World Bank itself.) In fact, it is well-known that since the headcount ratio of poverty is a non-decreasing function of the poverty line, most governments, especially the governments of poorer nations, would be reluctant to set the poverty line at realistic (leave alone generous) levels. India's is a particularly salient case in point, one that has been discussed at some painfully elaborate length in the preceding chapter of this book, and so requires no additional attention here.

Finally, in speaking of 'destitution lines', one is not committed, in a literal-minded way, to what Ravallion (2008) calls 'a life-threateningly low level of living'. I note that this is one dictionary definition of 'destitution': Merriam–Webster Online refers to destitution as 'such extreme want as to threaten life unless relieved.' However, there are alternative ways of conceptualizing destitution, as pointed out by Devereux (2003). In one such conceptualization, which Devereux (ibid.: 10) attributes to Craig and Porter (2003), '…lack of access to affordable, effective health care is dreaded, not just as a source of "ill health", important though that is, but as a source of vulnerability and, ultimately, destitution.' Such a conceptualization, in view of our earlier discussion, especially in the final section of Chapter 3, of official Indian poverty lines, which are close enough to the World Bank's line, in relation to the requirements of meeting fairly basic needs, renders the use of the term 'destitution lines' a not extravagant description even by the Merriam–Webster definition of the word in question. The term acquires even greater plausibility with reference to the construal by Dasgupta (1993: viii) of destitution as 'an extreme condition of ill-being', or by the *American Heritage Dictionary of the English Language* as 'a deprivation or lack; a deficiency'. In any event, the issue does not turn on a semantic dissection of the word 'destitution', so much as on the socio-economic import of the notion, read in context. In the end, the issue reduces to advancing the claim of a simple but serious point: in fixing poverty lines—an exercise which requires us to assess the needs of the poor—let us, please, not be excessively stoical and Spartan on behalf of the poor.

Poverty Comparisons across Space

Second, Reddy and Pogge (2010) allude to two problems of cross-section comparability occasioned by the use of PPP exchange rates, which may be summarized as, respectively, the 'irrelevant countries problem' and the 'irrelevant commodities problem' (see EPW 2008). That is, PPP exchange rates may be infected by prices of irrelevant commodities (non-essentials, on which the poor would typically spend a smaller proportion of their income than the general population), and also by prices and consumption patterns of irrelevant countries (those of the base country and, possibly, those of uninvolved third countries in bilateral comparisons between a pair of countries). Ravallion (2008) is right to point out that the latest World Bank estimates of global poverty have not been totally impervious to the possible merits of what one may call 'PPPs for the poor' (or PPPPs, for short). From what one can understand, the conversion rates employed continue to be PPPs which, apparently on the basis of some applied sensitivity analysis, have been judged to be not unacceptable proxies for PPPPs. Overall, one supposes that it should be possible to agree that PPPPs, if faithfully implemented, would constitute an improvement on PPPs. This said, it would be fair to observe that the use of PPPPs in place of PPPs would, in some measure, address only the 'irrelevant commodities' problem, not the 'irrelevant countries' problem: as such, it would at best (and subject to proper implementation) be a partial response to the issue of cross-sectional comparability, geared towards mitigation, rather than elimination, of a difficulty.

More fundamentally, given that the use of price indices is seldom unproblematic, there is a case for employing a defensible procedure of poverty comparisons that does not rely on the employment of price indices at all. This focuses directly on the issue of the 'common standard' according to which poverty comparisons are most meaningfully effected. Reddy and

Pogge (2010), Reddy (2004), and Subramanian (2005, 2009b) all point to the conceptual soundness of locating the 'common standard' in an identified set of basic human capabilities to function (as opposed to alternative proposals that have been made of locating the common standard in an identified commodity bundle or an identified level of 'real income'). For any given region at any given point of time, the poverty line can be taken to be the monetary resources that will be needed to achieve some minimally acceptable level of functionings deemed necessary to avoid capability deprivation. This could be Rs x in India and \$$y$ in the US (per appropriately defined unit of time). If the world consisted only of these two countries, the global headcount of poverty would be the sum of the Indian population with incomes less than Rs x and the US population with incomes less than \$$y$. The procedure, as one can see, does not require the use of any price indices. I am not suggesting this is a practically easy route to identification, but this fact does not entail accepting that practically feasible solutions which are conceptually unsound constitute a satisfactory resolution of the problem.

105

Inter-temporal Poverty Comparisons

Third, and as has been repeatedly stressed, poverty comparisons are meaningful only if a 'common standard' of comparison is employed. Consider the following illustrative exercise, which exemplifies a problem of inter-temporal comparability of poverty. Again, I quote, with some minor liberties, from EPW (2008: 5, 6):

> Suppose $1.25 per day at 2005 PPP is taken as the poverty line. In country X, whose local unit of currency is, say, 'klongs', suppose 30 klongs is equivalent to $1.25 in terms of the PPP exchange rate in 2005. Suppose 25 per cent of country X's population lives below the poverty line of 30 klongs in 2005. Suppose further that, using 2005 as the base year (2005 = 100), country X's consumer price index in 1993 is 75; then the 30 klongs poverty line in 2005 would have to be seen as being equivalent to a poverty line of 22.5 klongs ($= 0.75 \times 30$) at 1993 prices. Suppose 30 per cent of the population in country X lived below a poverty line of 22.5 klongs in 1993. Then, the World Bank methodology would have it that poverty in country X has declined from 30 per cent in 1993 to 25 per cent in 2005. By the same token, if the US consumer price index was 80 in 1993 (with 2005 as the base year), the

$1.25 poverty line, in equivalent terms for 1993 in the U.S., would be $1 (= 0.8×1.25). But notice that, by definition of the poverty line, one US dollar would have to be equivalent to 22.5 klongs in 1993 PPP— which may happen only and entirely by fluke! We have a consistency problem here. Trend analyses of global poverty estimates predicated on such inconsistency are essentially un-interpretable: the difficulty arises from the failure to employ any meaningfully common standard of poverty comparison. This, then, effectively queers the pitch for time-series comparisons.

Ravallion (2008: 78) responds to the above criticism in the following terms:

> Our method—let us call it method A—entails converting the international poverty line to local currencies using the PPP at the benchmark year... (now 2005) and then adjusting over time using the country's consumer price index (CPI) to get to the prices prevailing in the relevant survey year. The editorial claims that it would only be a 'fluke' if our method gave the same result if instead we had used the obvious alternative, method B, of converting all country-distributions to $ and then made the poverty calculations adjusting for inflation in the US.

107

It is not clear why Method B is the 'obvious alternative' to Method A, nor that the editorial has claimed that it is only by fluke that methods A and B will 'give the same result'! This makes it difficult to agree with the charge of a mistake having been made in the editorial (Ravallion 2008: 78–9):

> The mistake made in the editorial (and by one or two other critics) is not to realize that if one uses method B then the PPP for the non-benchmark year must be calculated consistently with the differential rates of inflation between the US and the country in question.

Specifically, the criticism made in the editorial in question does not undertake any comparison between Methods A and B. For, why would Method B be the 'obvious alternative' to Method A, unless inflation in the US was the same as the inflation in every other country? And if such an identity of inflation rates did in fact obtain, then B would not be an 'alternative' to A, B would just be indistinguishable from A! When Ravallion (2008: 78–9) says that 'the PPP for the non-benchmark year must be calculated consistently with the differential rates of inflation between the US and the country in question', one takes it he means the following. Suppose in the benchmark year—call it t_1—1 US\$ $\equiv$ Rupees x in terms of the PPP exchange rate. Suppose in some other, non-benchmark year—call it t_2—the price level has risen by 20 per cent vis-à-vis t_1 in the US and by 25 per cent in India. Ravallion's requirement, it seems, is that in year t_2, one must take it that 1.2 US \$ $\equiv$ Rupees $1.25x$, or (given that $1.25/1.2 = 1.042$), that 1 US\$ $\equiv$ Rupees $1.042x$. The editorial's claim is that it is only by fluke that the *actual* PPP in t_2 will turn out to be given by 1 US\$ $\equiv$ Rupees $1.042x$. The problem of consistency alluded to in the editorial is now simply explained. What if a survey was conducted in year t_2, and it was discovered that the PPP exchange rate for this year turns out to be: 1 US\$ $\equiv$ Rupees $1.05x$? Ravallion (2008: 79) effectively allows this possibility when he says: 'Granted, there may well be an inconsistency if one compares PPPs obtained from different benchmark years, for then consistency of the PPPs with the differential rates of inflation from the national CPIs is not assured (given differences in the quality of goods used and the weights)'. How then is the problem to be resolved? 'We follow standard practice in other international comparisons of only doing the PPP conversion for the benchmark year, and then making inter-temporal comparisons using the national data' (ibid.). What is being recommended, effectively, is that one must reject the t_2 survey result in the cause of 'consistent calculation'. But then, what if there is no reason to question the accuracy of either the t_1 or t_2 surveys? Must we sacrifice fact for consistency? If that is what is being recommended, then it is no longer true of t_2 that the poverty lines for the US and for India in dollars and rupees respectively reflect identically the same purchasing power, which violates precisely the cardinal property attributed to its IPL by the World Bank. (I may add that this problem of consistency would not ever 'surface' if one had information on PPP exchange rates *only* for the benchmark year; but then, empirical non-verifiability is not proof of the absence of analytical inconsistency!)

Of course, I do not dispute that an inconsistency will arise from comparison of PPPs from different benchmark years, let us call this mode of inter-temporal comparison Method C. Under Method C, we will have to forsake *horizontal* consistency, by which I mean that the actual relative rates of inflation between the US and the country in question will not be reflected in the

PPPs of the years under comparison. Under Method A, as we have seen, we will have to forsake *vertical* consistency, by which I mean that if the actual relative rates of inflation between the US and the country in question are preserved, then in the non-benchmark year the calculated PPP between the US and the country in question may not coincide with the actual PPP. It is in no way incidental to the problem of 'poverty identification' that failure to fix the poverty line in relation to some level of income explicitly derived from a common standard of human requirements, is linked to the problem that the analyst is constrained to resort to one or the other of Methods A and C of inter-temporal poverty comparison. Both methods, unfortunately, lead to inconsistent outcomes. One does not *have* to choose between the two inconsistencies, unless one has opted, for whatever reason, to confine one's universe of available identification-related alternatives to Methods A and C. Indeed, those not committed to 'dollar-a-day' type international poverty lines should not, as a matter of logic, be required to engage with this issue: in general, in a just world, one should be spared the necessity of dealing with a problem which is not of one's creation!

Poverty Trends: Artifacts or Reality?

Fourth, and as pointed out in EPW (2008), it turns out that the lower the poverty line employed, the more flattering is the resulting trend decline in poverty. This suggests that the trends we obtain are not so much a reflection of what is actually happening to poverty on the ground, as that they are a verification of the consistency of arithmetic. A substantively relevant consideration in this regard would be a tendency reported in Pogge (2008), and echoed in Reddy (2008): this is reflected in Table 4.1 reproduced from Pogge (2008) (itself based on data provided in Chen and Ravallion 2008).

Ravallion (2008: 79) states: 'The fact that we find that the rate of progress against poverty is slightly higher for \$1 per day than \$2 per day is hardly a sign that our results are arithmetic artifacts.' I submit that the choice of IPL is not anything as innocuous as this statement might suggest. Table 4.1 reveals that with an IPL of \$1 (2005 PPP), the world can claim to be 85 per cent ahead of schedule in realizing the Millennium Development Goal-1 (MDG-1); but with an IPL of \$2, the world would be found 68 per cent behind the

TABLE 4.1 MDG Achievement at Different International Poverty Lines

IPL Level in 2005 (US dollars)	1990 Baseline (millions of poor)	2005 Target Reduction of 27.5% (millions)	Annual Reduction Needed to Reach Target (%)	Reduction Needed to be 'On Track', 2005 (millions)	Actual Reduction Achieved, 1990–2005 (millions)	How is the World Doing with Regard to MDG-1? (100% = exactly on track)
$1.00/day	1303.2	358.4	1.28	228.7	424.2	185%, much ahead of schedule
$1.25/day	1817.5	499.8	1.28	318.9	417.9	131%, ahead of schedule
$2.00/day	2753.6	757.2	1.28	483.2	155.8	32%, much behind schedule
$2.50/day	3076.6	846.1	1.28	539.9	−63.6	−12%, regressing

Source: Pogge (2008).

warranted schedule for meeting MDG-1. The level at which the IPL is pitched is nothing if not crucial, and given a justifiable absence of extreme aversion to a Type I error, the \$2.50 IPL should be seen to be more reasonable than the \$1.25 IPL.

Or so one could argue if one's interest in the matter led one in that direction, and if one also suspected that the cumulative density function (cdf) of income had a tendency to behave over time as shown in Figure 4.1. If the rate of growth of low income levels was faster than that of high income levels, then it is conceivable that the cdfs in an initial period t_1 and in a later period t_2 could be as pictured in the figure. If one knew or suspected this to be the case, and if one also wished to demonstrate a deterioration in poverty, then one would have a strategic reason for pitching the poverty line at a 'high' level like z_H, to the right of z^* in the figure and one could proceed to seek a rationalization of z_H after the event. If one's interests ran in precisely the opposite direction, one might be inclined to pitch the poverty line at a 'low' level like z_L, to the left of z^* in the figure and thereafter invent reasons for finding z_L to be a plausible poverty line. In either case, one would be confirming the consistency

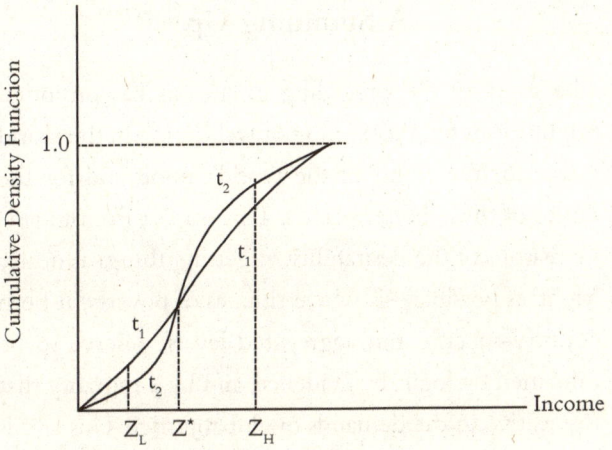

Between t_1 and t_2:
the headcount ratio declines when the poverty line is Z_L;
the headcount ratio increases when the poverty line is Z_H.

FIGURE 4.1 How Poverty Trends can Change Depending on where the Poverty Line is Pitched

of arithmetic rather than describing what is actually happening to poverty on the ground. Cynical? Perhaps. Wary? Definitely. The allusion to arithmetical artifacts and reality is amenable to interpretation as simply a rational invitation, addressed to each one of us that has a stake in national and international economic justice, to adopt a posture of wariness and vigilance towards vital statistics on national and international poverty.

A Summing Up

The topic of the preceding discussion has profound implications for a reckoning of well-being in the world today; for the rights of the world's poor; and for the duties of those better placed. This—apart from intrinsic reasons of the desirability of getting things as nearly 'right' as possible—is why estimates of poverty, at both country-specific and aggregated levels, deserve to be informed by logic, by evidence, and by a morality that is sensitive to the demands of global justice. This also is why the present debate is often difficult, occasionally charged, and unfailingly important.

5

The Source of the Difficulty
An Attempt at Elucidation

The Logic of the Problem

This chapter will aim to clarify the source of various confusions and controversies that have attended the identification exercise in different actual contexts that have been described in the preceding two chapters. The attempt at elucidation will entail some repetition of certain conceptual issues that have been discussed in Chapter 2. I am afraid this is to some extent unavoidable in an exposition of the present type, though it is also fair to issue the warning that this could slow things down for the reader who is in a hurry. I trust this prefatory remark will at least prepare readers for how they may wish to approach the chapter: the impatient ones may wish to skim through it, while others may prefer to plod along with the author. The first section draws heavily on Subramanian (2011b).

When we compare the magnitude of poverty (in terms, for example, of the headcount ratio) across space or over time, it is clear that, for the comparison to be meaningful, one requires that the poverty standard, in terms of which the poor are identified and poverty is measured, be invariant in the regimes under comparison. The crucial conceptual question that requires answering is: which is the logically most appropriate domain in which to demand the required invariance? Our review of the Indian, the US, and the World Bank experiences suggests that, typically, the invariance in question has been sought in the space of commodity bundles or real incomes. (By way of clarification, the term 'real income', as used here, will refer simply to 'income at constant prices', or 'income corrected for price changes'.) Thus, both the 1993 and the 2009 Expert Groups in India have advocated the employment of a normative 'poverty line commodity bundle', which will be valued at ruling prices to obtain space-/ time-specific nominal poverty lines. In the US Federal Government's official approach, one has a 'food plan' basket—one component of the poverty norm—which is required to be 'updated' every once a decade to take account of contemporaneous patterns of food consumption; the second (non-food) component is obtained by multiplying the money value of the food component by the reciprocal of the share of total income spent on food, a statistic which also is to be revised once every decade to take account of the empirical trends revealed by this statistic in the country's decennial food consumption surveys; and for the years within each decade, the base year poverty line will simply be corrected for price changes by employment of an appropriate consumer price index (CPI). The World Bank specifies a poverty line which is essentially a prescribed level of real income, captured in the 'dollar a day' formula. In general, then, it would appear that extant approaches to the identification problem have, by and large, tended to specify the money-metric poverty line in terms of the monetary value of a certain fixed and unique normative level of *resources* which is seen as separating the poor from the non-poor segments of a population.

A major insight afforded by Amartya Sen's perspective on the problem (Sen 1983) is the view that it is most sensible to adopt an absolute conception of poverty in the space of *functionings*, a functioning being a state of being or doing. For example, the requirements of avoiding hunger, ill health, lack of mobility and ignorance, and of appearing in public without shame, can all be specified in an absolute sense in the space of functionings. But these invariant requirements in the space of functionings could call forth very different requirements in terms of resources (commodities or incomes for instance). This could be because of heterogeneities amongst individuals: a physically handicapped individual would typically require more resources than one who is not so handicapped in order to achieve the same level of mobility; a person who is socially handicapped by the stigma of caste would typically require more resources than one who is not so disadvantaged in order to achieve the same level of social acceptance and inclusion. Or this could be because of differences across contexts: people living in cold countries would typically require more resources to be expended on warm clothing than people living in temperate climates in order to achieve the same level of protection against the effects of inclemency of the elements. The examples can be readily multiplied, but what they add up to is the validity of Sen's suggestion that absolute deprivation in the space of functionings is compatible with relative deprivation in the space of resources (of which commodities and incomes are examples).

If Sen's insight is taken seriously, then a general approach to the identification problem would consist in first setting out a list of functionings in respect of which absolute deprivation must be avoided so that a person may be certified as having escaped poverty; to specify the monetary cost of avoiding deprivation with respect to each of the listed functionings; and to aggregate these costs in order to arrive at a money-metric poverty line. In principle, the poverty line would have to be computed separately for each individual (to reflect relevant interpersonal variations in the ability to convert resources into functionings). To keep the problem practically tractable, one may wish to define only group-specific poverty lines (on the basis of the geographical region of origin, for instance). The procedure advocated here has the (conceptual) advantage of dispensing altogether with the need for employing price indices for the purpose of 'updating' poverty lines: the choice of price index has played no small part in the controversies of spatial and temporal comparability of poverty estimates, as evidenced in the literature on both India's poverty performance and the World Bank's estimates of global poverty.

What drives the 'functionings-based' approach to poverty identification, as we have seen, is the fact of interpersonal or cross-contextual variations in the ability to convert resources into functionings. But it is important to note that this very source of distinctiveness of the approach could also well be its undoing from a pragmatic point of view. Take the case of India, for instance. To secure some desired measure of discrimination that militates against the present practice of employing a unique money-metric poverty line (corrected only for price variations) for the entire country, it may be desirable—resorting to geographical disaggregation—to have at least one poverty line for each district of the Indian Union. Given upward of 600 districts in India, this would entail specifying 600 poverty lines for the country at any given point of time—a task that cannot readily be imagined to be an easy task for the planning and monitoring agencies of any country. This problem of 'feasibility' requires serious consideration, and in particular, it may signal the need for the setting up of a permanent Poverty Identification and Monitoring Bureau entrusted with the task of coming up with a set of reasonably realistic poverty lines for the country (see Reddy 2007). Without understating the magnitude of the task, it also bears remarking that one can overstate the onerousness of the exercise of a geographically disaggregated and commonsense costing of essential requirements of food, clothing, shelter, education, and health that should go into the making of a reasonable lower bound on the poverty line.

One suspects that most practitioners would endorse the conceptual soundness of the 'functionings approach' to the poverty identification problem, but are deterred from implementing it precisely because of the practical difficulty of doing so. What is clearly easier to implement is a view of identification in which what is held invariant across comparison regimes is commodity bundles or real incomes. Having resorted to a feasible approach to identification, there is probably a tendency also to rationalize the outcome as being conceptually sound. However, such a tendency is vulnerable to a problem of logic, which is easily enough recognized once it is brought out into the open, but which is nevertheless seldom openly acknowledged. This logical problem can be described (see Subramanian 2011b) along the following lines.

As we have seen, many extant approaches to money-metric poverty identification would endorse the following principle, which we could call Axiom 1.

Axiom 1. Other things remaining the same, a person who is certified to be non-poor in some time period 1 must continue to be deemed non-poor in some other time period 2 if his real income in Period 2 is greater than in Period 1, or, more demandingly, if his nominal income increases with no change in prices (the equivalent of an outward shift of the budget line in a two-commodities world).

Practitioners who subscribe to Axiom 1 are also unlikely to resist what we have called the 'functionings approach' to poverty identification. This approach can be summarized in terms of what I call Axiom 2.

Axiom 2. A person must be considered poor if his income is insufficient to achieve an identified set of functionings considered necessary in order to avoid deprivation.

The problem is that Axioms 1 and 2 are not mutually compatible (Subramanian 2011b). It is important to emphasize that it is not one's claim that there exist actual, identifiable, named, flesh-and-blood individuals who have claimed the rightness of both Axioms 1 and 2 simultaneously. Rather, one is inviting a thought experiment in which analysts are imagined to be presented with Axioms 1 and 2 at different points of time (separated by a gap long enough to deny memory any role in the matter): it is plausible that the analysts will endorse both axioms. For instance, it is widely believed that 'first-order stochastic dominance' is a sufficient guarantor of an unambiguous poverty judgment about the headcount ratio, in the following sense: if the cumulative density function of Distribution A lies somewhere below and nowhere above the cumulative density function of Distribution B, then one can claim unambiguously that poverty as measured by the headcount ratio is no greater in Distribution A than in Distribution B, no matter what (positive) poverty line is employed. It is not readily apparent that subscription to this view will go hand-in-hand with opposition to the 'functionings approach' to identification. Yet, logically, the stochastic dominance result ought, typically, not to be persuasive to a votary of the 'functionings approach': for note that the result requires that the poverty line employed be the same for both distributions, whereas, under the 'functionings approach', the poverty line for Distribution A could be so much higher than the poverty line for Distribution B that the headcount ratio for Distribution A could actually be higher than for Distribution B even though A first-order stochastically dominates B. To see how Axioms 1 and 2 could conflict with each other, consider the following simple example.

Suppose one takes rice and cloth to be commodities essential for achieving the functionings of avoiding hunger and appearing in public without shame. Consider a two-commodity world comprising rice and cloth, and two points of time, 1 and 2, in which the prices of the commodities remain unchanged, at Rs 2 per kilogram for rice and Rs 5 per yard for cloth. Suppose that, in Period 1, it is determined that 5 kilograms of rice are needed to avoid hunger and that 2 yards of cloth are required to appear in public without shame. Then, by Axiom 1, the money-metric poverty line in Period 1 would be Rs 20 (with Rs 10 needed to be spent on rice and Rs 10 on cloth). In Period 2, let us suppose that less rice and more cloth are needed to escape deprivation (perhaps because the nature of work has become less manual and because the prevailing norms require more clothing to avoid shame): let us assume that the normative requirements of the two commodities in Period 2 are 4 kilograms of rice and 3 yards of cloth respectively. Valued at Rs 2 per kilogram of rice and Rs 5 per yard of cloth, the money-metric poverty line under the 'functionings approach' would be Rs 23 in Period 2. Imagine a person j with an income of Rs 21 in Period 1 and of Rs 22 in Period 2. (These are also his real incomes in the two time periods, since prices have been assumed to remain constant.) Then, since j's income (Rs 22) falls short of the poverty line in Period 2 (Rs 23), j is poor in Period 2 according to Axiom 2. However, since j's income is in excess of the poverty line in Period 1, he is non-poor in Period 1 by Axiom 2, and since his real income has actually increased (to Rs 22) in Period 2, he is non-poor in Period 2 by Axiom 1. Subscribing to both Axioms 1 and 2 yields the contradictory result that person j is both poor and non-poor in Period 2.

Much of the confusion presiding over the various identification methodologies that have been reviewed in earlier sections can, I believe, be traced to a failure to explicitly acknowledge that principles of identification such as those captured in Axioms 1 and 2 are actually mutually incompatible; that the conceptually sound approach to the identification problem is the one constituted by what I have called the 'functionings approach'; and that other approaches, involving invariance of the poverty standard in the space of real incomes or of commodity bundles, are conceptually dubious ways of reckoning a money-metric poverty line. To put things briefly, it would appear that the conceptually sound approach to identification is handicapped by practical difficulties of implementation; and that conceptually doubtful approaches have tended to be deployed, without a proper acknowledgement of their logical inadequacies, simply because of the enormously greater practical ease of their implementation. What is sound is seen to be infeasible, and what is feasible is unsound. This must account in no small part for the generally unsatisfactory state of the conventional identification-followed-by-aggregation approach to the measurement of money-metric poverty.

Pending the implementation of some serious institutional arrangement for specifying a set of realistic country-wide poverty lines—such an institutional arrangement could take the form of a permanent Poverty Identification and Monitoring Bureau as has been alluded to earlier—is there a case for an alternative approach to tracking a 'pure' income-related poverty indicator? This problem is considered in the following section (which relies heavily on Subramanian 2009, 2010, 2011a).

The Quintile Income Statistic

In view of the severe difficulties posed by the identification problem, as reviewed in much of the preceding discussion, it is reasonable to ask if there may be an alternative approach to assessing income-related deprivation, one that bypasses the identification exercise altogether. The objective is not so much to present a wholly defensible *index* of poverty, as to advance a purely income-related *indicator* of poverty, one that can be employed to monitor the income-performance of the lower tail of an income distribution. The problem has been considered in Subramanian (2009b, 2011a), who shows that certain real-valued indices of welfare advanced in the literature can actually be justified as fuzzy poverty indices. I do not get into the details of derivation here, but rather I advance one such particular measure. This measure (which can also be rationalized as a fuzzy poverty indicator) is in my view a useful summary route to conceptualizing an aspect of poverty that comprehends also the interesting policy objective of what has been called 'pro-poor growth' (or 'inclusive growth' more generally). The measure was originally advanced by Kaushik Basu (2001, 2006), and he refers to it as the 'quintile income', which is just the average income of the poorest 20 per cent of the population. I suggest that—despite the fact that it has its own conceptual difficulties—the quintile income measure has something to commend it, from the following considerations: (a) it *can* be justified as a poverty indicator, albeit from 'fuzzy' considerations (Subramanian 2009b); (b) more directly, its concern with income-poverty *simpliciter* is apparent from its concern with the income status of the poorest 20 per cent of the population; (c) its meaning is easy to comprehend, and it can also be related to the notion of 'pro-poor growth' in a fashion that will be explained below; and (d) though it does have conceptual limitations of its own, it is not clear that these are more crippling than those which attend the conventional identification-cum-aggregation approach to poverty measurement.

One pernicious consequence of the conventional approach to poverty measurement is that the identification exercise affords an enormous license for the manipulation of the poverty line in order to secure this or that end (high or low magnitudes of poverty, as the case may be; or sharply declining, or slowly declining, or increasing trends, as the case may be). We have seen empirical instances, in the preceding review, of how the choice of poverty line can influence these crucial aspects of diagnosis of performance on the poverty front. This has implications, as noted earlier, for trends in money-metric poverty in India (the official estimates from 1977–8 suggest a pleasing trend decline, while Utsa Patnaik makes out a case for an *increasing* trend, on the bases, respectively, of choices of sets of poverty lines which cannot be privileged, one over the other, on the strength of superior intrinsic plausibility). Similarly, the choice of an International Poverty Line has critical implications for whether or not the world is on track in the matter of meeting its poverty-related Millennium Development Goal (MDG). A statistic like the quintile income is at least exempt from these sorts of problems of both diagnosis and manipulation.

To see how the quintile income may be useful in assessing and tracking poverty, consider the data on the growth rate of per capita average consumption expenditure in rural India from 1977–8 to 2004–5. Some of the information on trends in the mean consumption (call it μ) and in the quintile income (call it μ^Q) are available in Tables 2 and 3 of Subramanian (2009b), whose own computations are based on the relevant NSSO Consumption Expenditure Surveys. Employing the Consumer Price Index for Agricultural Labourers (CPI-AL) as a price deflator, it turns out that the mean per capita consumption expenditure μ in 1977–8 (respectively, 2004–5) at 1977–8 prices was Rs 68.89 (respectively, Rs 90.35), while the corresponding figures for the quintile income μ^Q were, respectively, Rs 29.14 and Rs 44.91. The compound annual rate of growth in μ over the 27-year period 1977–8 to 2004–5 is 1.01 per cent, while the corresponding growth rate for μ^Q is 1.62 per cent. It might appear that the definitely higher growth rate of μ^Q compared to that of

132

μ is a symptom of considerably egalitarian or inclusive growth, but before we come to that conclusion, it is instructive also to take into account the *base* with respect to which growth rates are computed: consider the case of a two-person distribution (1,100) in Period 1 which becomes (2,105) in Period 2—five-sixths of the additional income generated goes to the richer person, though the growth rate of his income is only 5 per cent, while the growth rate of the poorer person's income is 100 per cent!

In assessing what might constitute 'pro-poor growth', it is useful to consider, by way of analogy, the problem of optimal budgetary intervention in poverty alleviation schemes. The problem in question is then to identify the poverty-minimizing pattern of allocation of a fixed budget among the poor, subject to the constraint that no one receives a sum in excess of her poverty gap, and no poor person is taxed. The solutions to this problem would obviously depend upon the objective function—here subsumed in the poverty measure. Without getting into the details of the solutions to this programming problem, it is useful to note that the class of '*egalitarian*' solutions is constituted by those outcomes for which the poorer of two poor

133

individuals never gets a smaller share of the budget. The least egalitarian of the egalitarian outcomes then would be one in which each person receives an equal share of the budgetary provision available. (Contrast this with the more egalitarian outcome in which the poor receive transfers in proportion to their shortfalls from the poverty line; an even more equality-embracing outcome is the so-called lexicographic maximin solution in which, starting with the poorest of the poor, we have a sequence of progressive and income-equalizing transfers until all the poor are raised to the maximum income compatible with the size of the budget, with the rest receiving no transfer at all.)

In a similar spirit, consider an economy with a population of n_1 and a mean income of μ_1 in Period 1, which increase, respectively, to a population of n_2 and a mean income of μ_2 in Period 2. The aggregate incomes in the two periods are then, respectively, $Y_1 = n_1 \mu_1$ and $Y_2 = n_2 \mu_2$, and let the increase in aggregate income be denoted by $\Delta \, (\equiv Y_2 - Y_1)$. We can imagine we are in a situation similar to the problem of optimal budgetary intervention for poverty alleviation. We can ask: of all the possible 'egalitarian' distributions of Δ (which can be regarded as the fruit of growth), which is the least egalitarian? (By an 'egalitarian distribution of Δ' we simply mean one in which the poorer of two quantiles never receives a smaller share of the fruit of growth.) Suppose we decide, as a practical matter of convenience, to divide the population into quintiles. Then, the least egalitarian of the 'egalitarian' or (interchangeably) 'pro-poor' stratagems of distribution of Δ is one in which each quintile receives a share of $\Delta/5$. (This is a weakened version of what Klasen [2008] calls 'strong absolute pro-poor growth'.)

Applying these considerations to the data on quintile income, and using information on the size of India's rural population from the *Provisional Population Tables of the Census of India 2001*, we can perform certain computations which suggest that the compound annual rate of growth of the quintile income which would be compatible with the poorest quintile receiving a fifth share of the aggregate growth in income between 1977–8 and 2004–5 is of the order of 3.03 per cent. Call this the 'warranted' rate of growth in the quintile income. The calculations required to derive the 'warranted' growth rate are simple but tedious, and so have been relegated to an appendix (Appendix A3; see also Subramanian 2011a for details). While the 'warranted' compound annual rate of growth of the quintile income over the 27-year period from 1977–8 to 2004–5 is, as we have just seen, a modest 3.03 per cent, the actual growth rate, at 1.62 per cent, was even more modest— just about 54 per cent of the warranted growth rate. It is worth noting that what we call the warranted or desired growth rate is just the least egalitarian of the class of egalitarian distributions of the fruit of growth available. These findings, it would be fair to suggest, confirm what one would suspect to be a reasonably accurate description of the country's experience with income poverty: namely that of a slow and plodding climb out of considerable income deprivation—which is very different both from buoyant official estimates of significant rates of decline of poverty and profoundly pessimistic accounts of increasing poverty.

Briefly, there may be something to be said for measuring a money-metric indicator of poverty in terms of the quintile income, and of monitoring its performance by setting targeted rates of growth for the quintile income, in accordance with clearly articulated patterns of pro-poor distribution of the anticipated fruit of growth. The claim is not that such a view of poverty is exempt from conceptual niggles. But neither is the more conventional approach of identification and aggregation so exempt. Apart from this, the alternative proposal is amenable to simple and straightforward interpretation; it incorporates a workable notion of 'inclusive growth'; and it is not vulnerable to the temptations of manipulation.

6

Conclusion

This final chapter draws considerably on Subramanian (2011c). Around the time this was being written (November 2011), there was an upsurge of public discussion on a number of interrelated issues revolving around official assessments of poverty, the linking of welfare entitlements to poverty status, the reasonableness of officially stipulated money-metric poverty lines, the relative virtues of universalization and targeting of welfare benefits, and the fiscal sustainability of increased public spending in the cause of poverty redress.

India's poverty line has been very much at the centre of this debate, following on an affidavit filed by the Planning Commission in response to certain clarifications sought by the Supreme Court. The Court's reservation about the adequacy, at today's prices, of the

Tendulkar Committee's rural and urban poverty lines for 2004–5 at 2004–5 prices has been sought to be addressed in the Planning Commission's affidavit by simply 'updating' the 2004–5 poverty lines to 2011 via the Consumer Price Index for Agricultural Labourers (CPI-AL) for the rural areas of the country, and the Consumer Price Index for Industrial Workers (CPI-IW) for the urban areas. This is the procedure by which the rural and urban poverty lines of, respectively, Rs 26 per person per day and Rs 32 per person per day have been arrived at—poverty lines that have achieved a measure of notoriety and ridicule in the public perception. Additionally, and citing the Tendulkar Committee *Report*, the Planning Commission affidavit upholds the adequacy of these poverty lines. Paragraph 5 of the affidavit states: 'The recommended poverty lines ensure the adequacy of actual private expenditure per capita near the poverty lines on food, education and health and the actual calories consumed are close to the revised calorie intake norm for urban areas and higher than the norm in rural areas.'

In the wake of the public outcry against these poverty norms, and in particular the opposition to linking welfare (especially food) entitlements to poverty caps derived from the headcount ratios of the population living below the rural and urban poverty lines stated above, it has been clarified by the Planning Commission that these lines will not be employed to cap entitlements. One hopes the clarification is seriously and sincerely intended. If it is, then at least one incentive for understating poverty through understated poverty lines would be eliminated. (It is instructive, in this regard, to recall that even the Tendulkar Committee's estimates were assessed as being too high for one specific welfare intervention on behalf of the poor, as reflected in the Prime Minister's expressed reservation, in 2010, over the Supreme Court's directive on free distribution of food grains to the poor: in his reckoning, it was unrealistic to expect that food grains could be delivered free to as many as 37 per cent of the Indian population—which, precisely, is the Tendulkar Committee's estimate of the national headcount ratio of poverty in 2004–5).

If the declared determination to dissociate welfare entitlements from poverty caps should afford a reprieve to the overriding concern of confining poverty estimates to 'manageable' magnitudes and trends, then this could pave the way for a somewhat more relaxed and rational consideration of the principles by which a money-metric poverty line might be derived (Chapter 2, Chapter 5). An important guiding principle in this regard is the elementary requirement of an unvarying poverty standard to be employed in poverty comparisons across space or over time. 'Resourcist' approaches to specifying a money-metric poverty line have generally tended to identify this unvarying poverty standard in some given level of 'real income' (that is, income corrected only for variations in price levels), or in some given basket of commodities (to be valued at the prices that are relevant for the context under examination). 'Capability-based' approaches, on the other hand, seek invariance of the poverty standard in some identified set of absolute capabilities, seen as being reflected in the achievement of a set of corresponding functionings, such as, for example, freedom from hunger, illiteracy, and ill health: the poverty line is then the total cost of achieving these functionings.

Viewing poverty as a capability deprivation is compatible with drawing a money-metric poverty line which is not unique across individuals or contexts/environments. Specifically, personal heterogeneities can be reflected in variations across individuals in the ability

141

to convert resources into functionings; similarly, variations across contexts and environments could also call forth variable resources to address the requirements of a given set of functionings. This is the basis for Amartya Sen's (1983) well-known observation to the effect that poverty postulated in an absolute sense in the space of functionings is compatible with relative, or variable, real incomes or commodity bundles or resources in general that are required to achieve these functionings. Sanjay Reddy (2004) presents a lucid explication of the principles underlying the capability-based approach to specifying a money-metric poverty line, and of the conceptual soundness of seeking invariance of the poverty standard in the space of functionings rather than in that of real incomes or commodity bundles.

Official approaches to the specification of a poverty line for India have unfortunately not been inspired by any easily discernible conceptual clarity underlying the identification exercise. In particular, it is hard to confer any meaningful interpretation on the official poverty lines—whether we speak of the lines derived from a methodology advanced by a 1993 Expert Group appointed by the Planning Commission or of the lines implied by the methodology advanced by the recent

Tendulkar Committee—as actually constituting the amount of income that would be required in order to achieve a set of basic pre-specified human functionings needed for escaping the condition of deprivation. Chapter 3 has been concerned with a detailed assessment of the Indian experience, against this background, with the specification of a national poverty line. Other salient examples of deviations from the 'capability/functioning' approach to the identification problem would include the methodologies adopted in this regard by the United States' Federal Government's 'poverty thresholds' and the World Bank's 'dollar-a-day' international poverty lines. These approaches have also been sought to be described and critically interpreted (Chapter 4).

Let me conclude by returning to a special focus on the Indian experience. The discussion of various identification-related issues in the book, at the levels of both principle and practice, suggest that there is good reason why official assessments of poverty have met with the sort of generalized public dissatisfaction that has been in evidence in the wake of the recent Planning Commission affidavit submitted to the Supreme Court. As we have seen, the identification methodologies advanced by successive Task Forces and Expert Groups have had little by way of logical appeal or outcome plausibility to commend them. A major cause for this must be attributed to the absence of any real effort made by our planning agencies to identify a set of reasonably spatially differentiated and discriminating poverty lines based on a costing of minimally satisfactory levels of functioning with respect to an agreed-upon list of basic human capabilities. The case for setting up a permanent Poverty Identification and Monitoring Bureau for this purpose presents itself (see Reddy 2007, and Chapter 5 of this book). There is also, of course, a strong case for a direct assessment of multidimensional poverty in functioning space, and an example of an exercise of this nature, for India, is available in Jayaraj and Subramanian (2009).

Meanwhile, and pending the derivation of a set of realistic capability-based poverty lines for the nation, if what one is after is a purely money-metric indicator of how the relatively income-poor sections of the population are faring, then it makes sense to get out of the standard identification-cum-aggregation mould of conventional poverty measurement. An alternative approach might be to track a statistic such as the 'quintile income', as has been suggested by Kaushik Basu (2001, 2006), which is just the average income (or consumption expenditure) of the poorest 20 per cent of a population. Subramanian (2011a) deals with the case for presenting an annual time-series of the quintile income in the *Economic Survey*, and of contrasting the actual achievement in this regard with targeted levels of the quintile income based on an appropriate reckoning of an inclusive and egalitarian pattern of overall and quintile growth. This should be a helpful stratagem for confining planning exercises and purely money-metric poverty-related assessments to the straight and narrow.

In any event, the worst possible stratagem for addressing the problem of poverty would be to seek to delude oneself and others by defining it out of existence through the mechanism of postulating unrealistically low and substantively meaningless poverty lines. The issue is of far too much moral gravity to be dealt with in such terms. Or, if that sounds needlessly high minded, there is still available to one the argument based on enlightened self-interest. For any democratically elected government in harness, taking poverty seriously should do little harm to the prospects of reelection to power.

Appendices

A1. The Effect on the Headcount Ratio of 'Adjusting' the Expenditure Distribution

In working out the temporal behaviour of the headcount ratio consequent upon 'adjusting' the expenditure distribution, it is useful to note a set of facts peculiar to the Indian situation of the time under discussion. These facts would include the following: (a) the ratio of the CSO (Central Statistical Organization) mean to the NSS (National Sample Survey) mean was lower in 1977–8 than in 1983–4, the two ratios being, respectively, 1.09 and 1.22; (b) the NSS distributions have displayed a certain stationarity in the real mean over time—the 1977–8 and 1983–4 means at 1960–1 prices, using the Consumer Price Index for Agricultural Labourers (CPI-AL) as price deflator, being, respectively, Rs 21.27 and Rs 21.54; and (c) the NSS distributions do not exhibit an increase in inequality in 1983–4 vis-à-vis 1977–8, the Gini coefficients of inequality in the two years being, respectively, 0.30 and 0.34 (which, with a bit of license, we can interpret in terms of inter-temporally unvarying Lorenz curves). Observations (a), (b), and (c) will be used in the following stylized examination of the consequences of working with 'adjusted' expenditure distributions.

Let $\mathbf{x} = (x_1, \ldots, x_i, \ldots, x_m)$ be an ordered m-vector of individual expenditure levels in Period 1, with $x_i \leq x_{i+1}$ ($i = 1, \ldots, m-1$). Let $\mathbf{y} = (y_1, \ldots, y_i, \ldots, y_n)$ be similarly defined for Period 2, with $n \neq m$, to take account of population change. The vectors $\mathbf{x}$ and $\mathbf{y}$ may be seen as corresponding to the NSS expenditure distributions in 1977–8 and 1983–4 respectively. Let the ratio of the CSO mean to the NSS mean in time periods 1 and 2 be denoted by δ_1 and δ_2 respectively, with $(1 <) \delta_1 < \delta_2$ in conformity with observation (a) made earlier. The 'adjusted' expenditure vectors in time periods 1 and 2 will then be given, respectively, by $\mathbf{x}^A = \delta_1 \mathbf{x}$ and $\mathbf{y}^A = \delta_2 \mathbf{y}$. Let λ be the ratio of the price level in Period 2 to the price level in Period 1, so that if z is the poverty line at current prices in Period 1, λz is the poverty line at current prices in Period 2. Letting $q(\mathbf{x}; z)$ and $q(\mathbf{y}; \lambda z)$ stand for the numbers of people in poverty corresponding to the NSS distributions in periods 1 and 2 respectively, given that the poverty lines at current prices in the two periods are z and λz respectively, the headcount ratios in the two periods can be written, respectively, as $q(\mathbf{x}; z)/m$ and $q(\mathbf{y}; \lambda z)/n$. Assuming a non-increasing change in the headcount ratio from Period 1 to Period 2, and a positive headcount ratio in Period 2, let σ_1 stand for the proportionate change over the two time periods, so that:

$$\sigma_1 = [(q(\mathbf{x}; z)/m) - (q(\mathbf{y}; \lambda z)/n)]/ \\ (q(\mathbf{x}; z)/m); 0 \leq \sigma_1 \leq 1 \qquad \text{(A1.1)}$$

Next, let $q(\mathbf{x}^A; z)$ and $q(\mathbf{y}^A; \lambda z)$ denote the numbers of people in poverty corresponding to the 'adjusted' expenditure distributions in periods 1 and 2 respectively, given that the poverty lines at current prices in the two periods are z and λz respectively. Note that if the x_i and the y_i in the vectors $\mathbf{x}$ and $\mathbf{y}$ are sufficiently 'densely packed'—this is awkward terminology, occasioned by the fact that we are dealing with discrete distributions—then it should follow straightaway that the headcount ratios corresponding to the 'adjusted' expenditure distributions will be smaller than those corresponding to the NSS distributions, that is, $q(\mathbf{x}^A; z)/m < q(\mathbf{x}; z)/m$ and $q(\mathbf{y}^A; \lambda z)/n < q(\mathbf{y}; \lambda z)/n$. (This is just a matter of first-order stochastic dominance.) Further, define the quantities β_1 and β_2 as follows:

$$\beta_1 = q(\mathbf{x}^A; z)/q(\mathbf{x}; z) \text{ and } \beta_2 = q(\mathbf{y}^A; \lambda z)/ \\ q(\mathbf{y}; \lambda z), \text{ with } \beta_1, \beta_2 < 1 \qquad \text{(A1.2)}$$

β_i $(i = 1, 2)$ is just the ratio of the headcount ratio corresponding to the adjusted expenditure vector to the headcount ratio corresponding to the NSS expenditure vector in time period i. What can we say of the relative magnitudes of β_1 and β_2?

In order to answer this question we take note of the fact that the slope of the Lorenz curve at any point corresponding to an expenditure level x is given by x/μ where μ is the mean of the distribution. At Period 1 prices, the poverty line is z, while at Period 2 prices, it is λz. If μ is the mean of the NSS distribution in Period 1 at Period 1 prices, then, in line with observation (b), $\lambda\mu$ is the mean of the NSS distribution in Period 2 at Period 2 prices. A somewhat stringent, and also inexact, if simplifying, translation of observation (c) would be to require that the Lorenz curves for the distributions **x** and **y** coincide. The headcount ratio corresponding to the 'adjusted' distribution $\mathbf{x}^A$ will then be given by the horizontal ordinate of that point on the Lorenz curve at which the slope of the curve is $z/\delta_1\mu$; similarly, the headcount ratio corresponding to the 'adjusted' distribution $\mathbf{y}^A$ will be given by the horizontal ordinate of that point on the Lorenz curve at which the slope of the curve is $\lambda z/\lambda\delta_2\mu$. Since, by assumption, the Lorenz curves for both distributions $\mathbf{x}^A$ and $\mathbf{y}^A$ coincide, and since $\delta_1 < \delta_2$ so that $z/\delta_1\mu > z/\delta_2\mu$, the point at which the slope of the Lorenz curve is greater (that is, at which the slope is $z/\delta_1\mu$) will be to the right of the point at which the slope is smaller (that is, at which the slope is $z/\delta_2\mu$). In other words, the headcount ratio corresponding to the distribution $\mathbf{x}^A$ will be closer (than the headcount ratio corresponding to the distribution $\mathbf{y}^A$) to the headcount ratio shared by the distributions **x** and **y**. That is to say, precisely, that β_1 will be greater than β_2.

Next, let σ_2 be the proportionate decline in the head-count ratios corresponding to the 'adjusted' expenditure vectors $\mathbf{x}^A$ and $\mathbf{y}^A$ over the periods 1 to 2:

$$\sigma_2 = [(q(\mathbf{x}^A; z)/m) - (q(\mathbf{y}^A; \lambda z)/n)]/(q(\mathbf{x}^A; z)/m) \quad \text{(A1.3)}$$

Making use of (A1.1), (A1.2), and (A1.3), a little bit of manipulation will yield:

$$\sigma_2 - \sigma_1 = (\beta_1 - \beta_2)(1 - \sigma_1)/\beta_1 \qquad \text{(A1.4)},$$

which is positive, since β_1, $(\beta_1 - \beta_2)$, and $(1 - \sigma_1)$ are all positive. We are now in a position to state the following proposition:

Proposition. Under the conditions discussed earlier, and other things remaining equal, (i) the headcount ratios correspond-ing to the 'adjusted' expenditure distributions will be smaller than those corresponding to the NSS distributions; and (ii) the proportionate decline over two time periods of the headcount ratio will be greater for the 'adjusted' than for the NSS distributions.

A2. Basic Demand Theory and Poverty Identification

As noted in the text, the 1993 Expert Group endorsed the 1979 Task Force's procedure of fixing the poverty line in 1973–4 in terms of the observed level of consumption expenditure at which the calorific norm was realized, and recommended that the poverty lines in subsequent years should be determined by simply revaluing the 1973–4 poverty line consumption bundle at current prices. The implications of this approach for the notion that the poverty line is uniformly anchored in a nutritional norm are examined in this Appendix. In particular, it will be shown that under plausible circumstances, and as one moves further away from the reference year 1973–4, the official poverty line may not be large enough to support a choice of nutritional attainment that will meet the norm of nutritional adequacy. The Appendix attempts to achieve its end by presenting a simple story of consumer behaviour—that of elementary textbook demand theory—in order to explain how the poverty line is derived in the reference year and determined in subsequent years. The ingredients of the story will be kept as simple as possible, so that the emphasis is only on the underlying logic and not on any complexity of needless detail.

With this in mind, it is postulated that there are only two goods in the economy, food (x) and non-food (y). It is assumed that the norm of nutritional adequacy can be fixed directly in terms of a desired quantity of x, which will be designated by x^0. The prices of food and non-food are p^x and p^y respectively. Income is represented by m. Every agent is assumed to possess a utility function U defined on the quantities of the two commodities she consumes: $U = U(x, y)$; and the customary restrictions on the first and second partial derivatives with respect to each of the arguments of the utility function will be assumed to hold, that is, U_x, $U_y > 0$ and U_{xx}, $U_{yy} < 0$. To make things even simpler, one can specialize the utility function to the familiar Cobb–Douglas form: $U(x, y) = x^\alpha y^{1-\alpha}$, $0 < \alpha < 1$. The agent's budget constraint is given by the equation $p^x x + p^y y = m$. The consumer is assumed to maximize his utility by appropriate choice of x and y, subject to his budget constraint. That is, he solves the following problem:

Maximize $U(x, y) = x^\alpha y^{1-\alpha}$
$\{x, y\}$ s.t. $p^x x + p^y y = m$.

An application of standard elementary optimization techniques will yield the following solution to the problem:

$$x^*(p^x, m) = \alpha m/p^x, \; y^* (p^y, m) = (1-\alpha)m/p^y \qquad (A2.1)$$

The poverty line is derived by computing that level of income (given the prices of the two commodities) at which it is optimal for the consumer to purchase the normatively prescribed quantity of food, x^0. Call this level of income m^*. Then, in view of (A2.1), it is immediate that:

$$m^* = x^0 p^x/\alpha \qquad (A2.2)$$

Further, and again in view of (A2.2), the optimal commodity bundle of the person with the poverty line income of m^* will be given by:

$$x^* (p^x, m^*) = x^0, \; y^* (p^y, m^*) = (1-\alpha)m^*/p^y \qquad (A2.3)$$

152

Let $t = 1$ be the reference year in which the poverty line is determined in relation to consumer behaviour, as described earlier. Using the subscript 1 to indicate that we are speaking of the reference year, (A2.3) can be rewritten as:

$$x_1^*(p_1^x, m_1^*) = x^0, \, y_1^*(p_1^y, m_1^*) = (1 - \alpha_1) m_1^* / p_1^y \quad \text{(A2.3')}$$

(A2.3') now represents the 'poverty commodity bundle': any level of income, in any other year, at which the commodity bundle $(x^0, (1 - \alpha_1) m_1^* / p_1^y)$ can be afforded, will be regarded to be sufficient to avoid poverty in that year. That is to say, if p_t^x and p_t^y are the respective prices of food and non-food in year t, and if Year 1 is employed as the 'reference' year, then the poverty line in year t at current prices—in accordance with the Planning Commission methodology—will be taken to be represented by the income level $m_t^0(1)$, defined as:

$$m_t^0(1) \equiv p_t^x x^0 + p_t^y (1 - \alpha_1) m_1^* / p_1^y \quad \text{(A2.4)}$$

Next, consider the two successive periods of time $t = 1$ and $t = 2$. Is there any guarantee that a person with a Period 2 income of $m_2^0(1) \equiv p_2^x x^0 + p_2^y (1 - \alpha_1) m_1^* / p_1^y$ (as in [A2.4]) will actually consume the nutritionally normative quantity x^0 of x in Period 2? No, not unless the factors which determine his optimal choice of x and y—namely his preferences and the relative prices of the two commodities—remain the same in Period 2 as in Period 1. We consider taste changes first, keeping prices and income fixed.

In particular, consider an individual for whom $p_2^x = p_1^x$, $p_2^y = p_1^y$, $m_2 = m_1 = m_1^*$, but $\alpha_2 < \alpha_1$, that is, the only thing which has changed in Period 2 vis-à-vis Period 1 is the shape of the individual's preference function: he now has a more urgent desire for non-food over food than previously, that is, the substitutability of food for non-food has declined. It is clear then that his optimal consumption of food in Period 2 (*vide* equation [A2.1]) will be given by:

$$x_2^* = \alpha_2 m_1^* / p_2^x = \alpha_2\, m_1^* / p_1^x \text{ (since } p_2^x = p_1^x$$
by assumption) $\hspace{3cm}$ (A2.5)

But we know from (A2.1) and (A2.3') that

$$x_1^* = \alpha_1 m_1^* / p_1^x = x^0 \hspace{3cm} \text{(A2.6)},$$

whence, in view of (A2.5) and (A2.6):

$$x_2^*/x^0 = \alpha_2/\alpha_1 < 1 \text{ since, } \textit{ex hypothesi, } \alpha_2 < \alpha_1 \hspace{1cm} \text{(A2.7)}$$

The 'dual' of the result in (A2.7) is that the income that will be required in Period 2 such that it would be optimal with this income to consume x^0 quantity of x, is greater than m_1^*. For, note from (A2.2) that the required income, call it m_2^*, is given by $m_2^* = x^0 p_2^x / \alpha_2 > m_1^* = x^0 p_1^x / \alpha_1$, since $\alpha_2 < \alpha_1$ (and $p_2^x = p_1^x$).

Next, we keep preferences and 'real' income constant and examine what happens with a change in relative prices. Specifically, imagine that the coefficient in the Cobb–Douglas utility function is the same, at α_1, in both periods 1 and 2; and that the price of food in Period 2 has increased faster than the price of non-food in Period 2, so that, say, $p_2^x = \rho p_1^x$ and $p_2^y = \gamma p_1^y$, with $\rho > \gamma > 1$. Consider an individual with income m_1^* in Period 1, which rises to a level m_2 in Period 2 such that the 'poverty line commodity bundle' of (x^0, y_1^*) is just exactly affordable at the Period 2 prices of x and y, p_2^x and p_2^y respectively. That is, we suppose that $m_2 = m_2^0(1) \equiv p_2^x x^0 + p_2^y (1-\alpha_1) m_1^*/p_1^y$ (see equation [A2.4]). Would this income suffice to ensure that the person will optimally consume x^0 quantity of x in Period 2? The answer is no, for, in view of (A2.1):

$x_2^* = \alpha_1 m_2/p_2^x = (\alpha_1/p_2^x) m_2^0(1) = (\alpha_1/p_2^x)[p_2^x x^0 + p_2^y (1-\alpha_1) m_1^*/p_1^y]$ (obtained by substituting for $m_2^0(1)$ from [A2.4]) $= (\alpha_1/p_2^x)[p_2^x x^0 + p_2^y (1-\alpha_1)(x^0 p_1^x/\alpha_1)/p_1^y]$ (obtained by substituting for m_1^* from [A2.2]) $= \alpha_1 x^0 + (1-\alpha_1)(p_1^x/p_2^x)(p_2^y/p_1^y)x^0 = [\alpha_1 + (1-\alpha_1)(\gamma/\rho)]x^0 < x^0$, since $\gamma < \rho$ by assumption. What is at work is just the 'substitution effect' of standard demand theory: at the optimum, less of the commodity whose price has risen faster, and more of the commodity whose price has risen more slowly, will be consumed. Further, the income required in Period 2 to permit x^0 quantity of x to be consumed optimally will be greater than $m_2^0(1)$: this income level, call it m_2^*, is given (see equation [A2.2] again) by:

$m_2^* = x^0 p_2^x/\alpha_1 = \rho x^0 p_1^x/\alpha_1 = \rho m_1^* > m_2^0(1) = [\rho\alpha + \gamma(1-\alpha)] m_1^*$, since $\rho > \gamma$.

There is another important issue to be considered in the present context: this has to do with the fact that certain non-food commodities which were initially 'free', in the sense, for instance, of belonging to a pool of common property resources, begin, over time, to become priced commodities that have to be purchased in the market (see Mehta and Venkatraman 2000). The case of firewood in the rural areas is a relevant example of the phenomenon under review. In terms of the analytical construct that has been employed here, it may be useful to think of the non-food commodity (y) as firewood fuel. Suppose a quantity y^0 of y is available 'free', as a common property resource. The consumer then has to pay a price p^y per unit of y only for every unit consumed in excess of y^0. The consumer's budget constraint then becomes: $p^x x + p^y \max[(y - y^0), 0] = m$, and his optimization problem can be written as:

Maximize $U(x, y) = x^\alpha y^{1-\alpha}$

$\{x, y\}$

s.t. $p^x x + p^y \max[(y - y^0), 0] = m$.

It can be verified that the optimal solution to this problem is given by:

$$x^\star(p^x, p^y, m) = (\alpha/p^x)(m + p^y y^0), \, y^\star(p^x, p^y, m) = y^0 + [(1-\alpha)/p^y]m \qquad (A2.8)$$

The poverty line, as before, is that level of income $m^\star$ at which (given the prices of the commodities), it is optimal for the consumer to purchase x^0 quantity of x, whence, in view of (A2.8), we have:

$$m^* = p^x x^0/\alpha - p^y y^0 \qquad (A2.9)$$

Employing the subscript 1 for the reference year, it follows from (A2.8) and (A2.9) that the 'poverty commodity bundle' in Year 1 is given by:

$$x_1^* (p_1^x, p_1^y, m_1^*) = x^0, y_1^* (p_1^x, p_1^y, m_1^*) =$$
$$y_1^0 + [(1-\alpha_1)/p_1^y]m_1^* \qquad (A2.10)$$

Suppose now that in Year 2 prices, income and tastes all remain the same as in Year 1, but that the availability of the common property resource has dwindled from y_1^0 to y_2^0, necessitating a greater dependence on the market for the consumption of y. In particular, we suppose that $p_1^x = p_2^x = p^x$ (say), $p_1^y = p_2^y = p^y$ (say), $m_2 = m_1^*$, $\alpha_1 = \alpha_2 = \alpha$ (say), and $y_2^0 < y_1^0$. It is clear, given this situation, that the poverty line income in Year 2 which is compatible with the official methodology is m_1^*, and that the optimal consumption of x in Year 2 will be given (in view of [A2.8]) by:

$$x_2^* (p_2^x, p_2^y, m_2) = (\alpha/p_x)(m_1^* + p^y y_2^0) < x^0 = (\alpha/p^x)(m_1^* + p^y y_1^0), \text{ since by assumption, } y_2^0 < y_1^0$$

Further, the income which will be required in Year 2 to induce optimal consumption of x^0 quantity of x will be greater than the poverty line level of income allowed by the official methodology, for, given (A2.9), one has:

$$m_2{}^* = p^x x^0/\alpha - p^y \gamma_2{}^0 > m_1{}^* = p^x x^0/\alpha - p^y \gamma_1{}^0, \text{ since } \gamma_2{}^0 < \gamma_1{}^0$$

A3. The 'Warranted' Rate of Growth in Quintile Income

Employing the notation defined in the text, and the subscripts 1 and 2 for the years 1977–8 and 2004–5 respectively, note that μ_1 = Rs 68.89 and μ_2 = Rs 90.35 (at 1977–8 prices). Census population figures suggest that n_1 = 496.87 millions and n_2 = 786.5 millions. It follows that $Y_1 (= n_1 \mu_1)$ = Rs 34,229 millions and $Y_2 (= n_2 \mu_2)$ = Rs 71,060 millions, whence $\Delta (\equiv Y_2 - Y_1)$ = Rs 36,830.91 millions. The share of Δ which should go to the poorest quintile, in terms of the least egalitarian of the 'inclusive' patterns of distribution, is $\Delta/5$, which works out to Rs 7,366.18 millions. The total income of the poorest quintile in 2004–5 ought then to be the sum of its equal share of the fruit of growth (Rs 7,366.18 millions) and its total income in 1977–8 (which is the product of the mean income Rs 29.14 of the poorest quintile and its population of 99.37 millions, which works out to Rs 2,895.64 millions.) The total 'desired' aggregate income of the poorest quintile in 2004–5 then is Rs 7,366.18 millions + Rs 2,895.64 millions = Rs 10,261.82 millions, whence the 'desired' mean income of the poorest quintile in

2004–5, given that its 2004–5 population is 157.3 millions, is Rs 65.24 (= 10,261.82/157.3). To summarize: the actual quintile incomes in 1977–8 and 2004–5, at 1977–8 prices, were Rs 29.14 and Rs 44.91. The 'desired' or 'warranted' quintile income in 2004–5, at 1977–8 prices, is Rs 65.24. The corresponding actual and 'warranted' compound annual rates of growth of the quintile income are, then, 1.01 per cent and 3.03 per cent respectively.

References

Ahluwalia, M.S. (1978), 'Rural Poverty and Agricultural Performance in India', *Journal of Development Studies*, 14(2): 298–323.

Bardhan, P.K. (1970), 'On the Minimum Level of Living and the Rural Poor', *Indian Economic Review*, 5(1): 129–36.

——— (1971), 'On the Minimum Level of Living and the Rural Poor: A Further Note', *Indian Economic Review*, 6(1): 78–87.

——— (1973), 'On the Incidence of Poverty in Rural India of the Sixties', *Economic and Political Weekly*, 8(4/6): 245–54.

Basu, K. (2001), 'On the Goals of Development', in G.M. Meier and J.E. Stiglitz (eds), *Frontiers of Development Economics: The Future in Perspective*. New York: Oxford University Press, pp. 61–86.

——— (2006), 'Globalization, Poverty, and Inequality: What is the Relationship? What Can Be Done?', *World Development*, 34(8): 1361–73.

Bhatty, I.Z. (1974), 'Inequality and Poverty in Rural India', in T.N. Srinivasan and P.K. Bardhan (eds), *Poverty and Income Distribution in India*. Calcutta: Statistical Publishing Society, pp. 291–336.

Calvo, C. and S. Dercon (2005), 'Measuring Individual Vulnerability', UNU-WIDER Jubilee Conference, Helsinki, Finland.

Chen, S. and M. Ravallion (2000), 'How Did the World's Poorest Fare in the 1990s?', Working Paper, August, World Bank, Washington, D.C. Available at http://ideas.repec.org/p/wbk/wbrwps/2409.html.

———— (2008), 'The Developing World is Poorer than We Thought, But No Less Successful in the Fight against Poverty', Policy Research Working Paper 4703, August, World Bank Development Research Group, World Bank, Washington, D.C.

Chiappero Martinetti, E. (1994), 'A New Approach to Evaluation of Well-being and Poverty by Fuzzy Set Theory', *Giornale Degli Economisti e Annali di Economia*, 53(7–9): 367–88.

Cornia, G.A. and F. Stewart (1995), 'Two Errors of Targeting', *Journal of International Development*, 5(5): 459–96.

Craig, D. and D. Porter (2003), 'Poverty Reduction Strategy Papers: A New Convergence', *World Development*, 31(1): 53–70 (also cited in Devereux [2002]).

Dandekar, V.M. and N. Rath (1971), *Poverty in India*. Pune: Indian School of Political Economy.

Dasgupta, P. (1993), *An Inquiry into Well-Being and Destitution*. Oxford: Clarendon Press.

Devereux, S. (2003), 'Conceptualizing Destitution', Institute of Development Studies Working Paper 216, Brighton, Sussex.

Duclos, J.Y. and A. Araar (2005), *Poverty and Equity: Measurement, Policy and Estimation with DAD*. New York: Springer. Available at http://web.idrc.ca/en/ev-97152-201-1-DO_TOPIC.html.

Economic and Political Weekly (EPW) (2008), 'How Many Poor in the World?', *Economic and Political Weekly*, 25 October, 43(43): 5–6.

Fisher, G.M. (1992), 'The Development and History of the Poverty Thresholds', *Social Security Bulletin*, 55(4): 3–14.

Government of India (2009), *Report on Conditions of Work and Promotion of Livelihoods in the Unorganized Sector*. New Delhi: National Commission for Enterprises in the Unorganized Sector.

Greer, J. and E. Thorbecke (1986), 'A Methodology for Measuring Food Poverty Applied to Kenya', *Journal of Development Economics*, 24(1): 59–74.

Groedhart, T., V. Halberstadt, A. Kapteyn, and B. van Praag (1977), 'The Poverty Line: Concept and Measurement', *Journal of Human Resources*, 12(4): 503–20.

Hagenaars, A. and B. van Praag (1985), 'A Synthesis of Poverty Line Definitions', *Review of Income and Wealth*, 31(2): 139–54.

Jayaraj, D. and S. Subramanian (2009), 'A Chakravarty-D'Ambrosio View of Multidimensional Deprivation: Some Estimates for India', *Economic and Political Weekly*, 45(6): 53–65.

Kapteyn, A., P. Kooreman, and R. Willemse (1988), 'Some Methodological Issues in the Implementation of Subjective Poverty Definitions', *Journal of Human Resources*, 23: 222–42.

Klasen, S. (2008), 'Economic Growth and Poverty Reduction: Measurement Issues Using Income and Non-Income Indicators', *World Development*, 36(3): 420–45.

Ligon, E. and L. Schechter (2003), 'Measuring Vulnerability', *Economic Journal*, 113(486): C95–C102.

Meenakshi, J.V. and B. Vishwanathan (2003), 'Calorie Deprivation in Rural India, 1983–1999/2000', *Economic and Political Weekly*, 38(4): 369–75.

Mehta, J. and S. Venkatraman (2000), 'Poverty Statistics: Barmicide's Feast', *Economic and Political Weekly*, 35(27): 2377–82.

Minhas, B.S. (1970), 'Rural Poverty, Land Redistribution and Development Strategy', *Indian Economic Review*, 5(1): 97–128.

——— (1971a), 'Rural Poverty and the Minimal Level of Living: A Reply', *Indian Economic Review*, 6(1): 69–77.

——— (1971b), 'More on Rural Poverty, or a Glimmer of Progress', *Indian Economic Review*, 6(1): 88–94.

Minhas, B.S. (1971c), 'Rural Poverty, Numbers Games and Polemics', *Indian Economic Review*, 6(1): 97–102.

Nayyar, R. (1991), *Rural Poverty in India: An Analysis of Inter-State Differences*. New Delhi: Oxford University Press.

Orshansky, M. (1965), 'Counting the Poor: Another Look at the Poverty Profile', *Social Security Bulletin*, 28(1): 3–29.

Osmani, S.R. (1992), 'On Some Controversies in the Measurement of Undernutrition', in S.R. Osmani (ed.), *Nutrition and Poverty*. Oxford: Clarendon Press, pp. 121–61.

Panda, M. and R.K. Rath (1999), 'Price Changes and Some Underlying Aspects of Measurement of Poverty', Indira Gandhi Institute of Development Research Discussion Paper No. 152, IGIDR, Mumbai.

Patnaik, U. (2004), 'The Republic of Hunger', *Social Scientist*, 32(9–10): 9–35. (Text of a Public Lecture on the Occasion of the 50th Birthday of Safdar Hashmi on 10 April 2004, New Delhi.)

————— (2007), 'Neoliberalism and Rural Poverty in India', *Economic and Political Weekly*, 48(32): 3132–50.

Planning Commission (1962), 'Perspective of Development: 1961–1976, Implications of Planning for a Minimum Level of Living', Government of India, New Delhi (Reprinted in Srinivasan and Bardhan [1974], *Poverty and Income Distribution*).

Planning Commission (1979), *Report of the Task Force on Projections of Minimum Needs and Effective Consumption Demand*. New Delhi: Government of India.

Planning Commission (1984), *Report of the Study Group on the Concepts and Estimation of Poverty Line*. New Delhi: Government of India.

———— (1985), *7th Five Year Plan* (Vol. I). New Delhi: Government of India.

———— (1993), *Report of the Expert Group on Estimation of Proportion and Number of Poor*. New Delhi: Government of India.

———— (2009), *Report of the Expert Group to Review the Methodology for Estimation of Poverty*. New Delhi: Government of India.

Pogge, T.W. (2008), 'Where the Line is Drawn: A Rejoinder to Ravallion', One-Pager Number 69, October. International Poverty Centre, United Nations Development Programme (UNDP), Brasilia.

Pogge, T.W. and S.G. Reddy (2006), 'Unknown: The Extent, Distribution and Trend of Global Income Poverty'. Available at http://www.columbia.edu/~sr793/povpop.pdf.

Qizilbash, M. (2003), 'Vague Language and Precise Measurement: The Case of Poverty', *Journal of Economic Methodology*, 10(1): 41–58.

Ravallion, M. (1998), 'Poverty Lines in Theory and Practice', Living Standards Measurement Study, Working Paper 133, World Bank, Washington, D.C.

———— (2004), 'Monitoring Progress against Global Poverty', *In Focus: Dollar a Day How Much Does it Say?*, September, 6–8, International Poverty Centre, UNDP, Brasilia.

———— (2008), '"How Many Poor in the World?": A Reply', *Economic and Political Weekly*, 43(45): 78–9.

———— (2010), 'How *Not* to Count the Poor? A Reply to Reddy and Pogge', in J. Stiglitz, S. Anand, and P. Segal (eds), *Debates in the Measurement of Poverty*. Oxford: Oxford University Press.

Ravallion, M., G. Datt, and D. van de Walle (1991), 'Quantifying Absolute Poverty in the Developing World', *Review of Income and Wealth*, 37(4): 345–61.

Ray, R. and G. Lancaster (2005), 'On Setting the Poverty Line Based on Estimated Nutrient Prices: Condition of Socially Disadvantaged Groups during the Reform Period', *Economic and Political Weekly*, Xl(1): 46–56.

Reddy, S.G. (2004), 'A Capability-based Approach to Estimating Global Poverty', *In Focus: Dollar a Day How Much Does it Say?*, September, 6–8, International Poverty Centre, UNDP, Brasilia.

———— (2007), 'The Great Indian Poverty Debate', *Development*, 50(2): 166–71.

Reddy, S.G. (2008), 'Differently Distorted: The World Bank's "Updated" Poverty Estimates', *Economic and Political Weekly*, 43(43): 44–7.

Reddy, S.G. and T.W. Pogge (2010), 'How *Not* to Count the Poor', in Stiglitz, Anand, and Segal (eds), *Debates in the Measurement of Poverty*. A longer version is available at www.socialanalysis.org.

Rudra, A. (1974), 'Minimum Level of Living—A Statistical Examination', in Srinivasan and Bardhan (eds), *Poverty and Income Distribution*.

Sen, A.K. (1983), 'Poor, Relatively Speaking', *Oxford Economic Papers*, 35(2): 153–69.

——— (1985a), *Commodities and Capabilities*. Amsterdam: North-Holland Press.

——— (1985b), 'A Sociological Approach to the Measurement of Poverty: A Reply to Professor Townsend', *Oxford Economic Papers*, 37(4): 669–76.

——— (1992), *Inequality Reexamined*. New York: Russell Sage Foundation and Oxford: Clarendon Press.

Shorrocks, A.F. (2004), 'Inequality and Welfare Evaluation of Heterogeneous Income Distributions', *Journal of Economic Inequality*, 2(3): 193–218.

——— (2005), 'Inequality Values and Unequal Shares', UNU-WIDER, Helsinki, Finland. Available at http://www.wider.unu.edu/conference/conference-2005-5/conference-2005.5.htm.

Shorrocks, A.F. and S. Subramanian (1994), 'Fuzzy Poverty Indices', Mimeo, University of Essex.

——— (2006), 'Poverty: An Overview', Mimeo, UNU-WIDER, Helsinki, Finland.

Srinivasan, T.N. and P.K. Bardhan (eds) (1974), *Poverty and Income Distribution in India*. Calcutta: Statistical Publishing Society.

Subramanian, S. (1987), 'Poverty Statistics: Real Phenomena or Arithmetical Illusions? A Note', in Malcolm S. Adiseshiah (ed.), *Mid-Year Review of the Economy 1986–87*. New Delhi: Lancer International, pp. 135–41.

——— (1990), 'Poverty', in Malcolm S. Adiseshiah (ed.), *Eighth Plan Perspectives*. New Delhi: Lancer International, pp. 221–54.

——— (1997), 'Introduction: The Measurement of Inequality and Poverty', in S. Subramanian (ed.), *Measurement of Inequality and Poverty* (Readers in Economics Series). New Delhi: Oxford University Press, pp. 1–53 (Reprinted as Oxford India Paperbacks: 2000, 2002).

——— (2005), 'Unravelling a Conceptual Muddle: India's Poverty Statistics in the Light of Basic Demand Theory', *Economic and Political Weekly*, XL(1): 57–66.

——— (2009a), '"How Many Poor in the World?": A Critique of Ravallion's Reply', *Economic and Political Weekly*, 44(5): 67–71.

——— (2009b), 'A Practical Proposal for Simplifying the Measurement of Income Poverty', in K. Basu and

R. Kanbur (eds), *Arguments for a Better World: Essays in Honour of Amartya Sen, Volume 1: Ethics, Welfare, and Measurement*. Clarendon: Oxford University Press, pp. 435–52.

Subramanian, S. (2010), 'Identifying the Income-Poor: Some Controversies in India and Elsewhere', Discussion Paper 46, Poverty, Equity and Growth Discussion Papers Series, Courant Research Centre, Goettingen, Germany.

————— (2011a), '"Inclusive Development" and the Quintile Income Statistic', *Economic and Political Weekly*, XLVI(4): 69–72.

————— (2011b), 'Money-metric Poverty Identification: A Cautionary Note', *Journal of Economic Analysis*, 2(1): 35–56.

————— (2011c), 'The Poverty Line: Getting it Wrong Again', *Economic and Political Weekly*, XLVI(49): 37–42.

Suryanarayana, M.H. (1996), 'Food Security and Calorie Adequacy Across States: Implications for Reforms', *Journal of Indian School of Political Economy*, 8(2): 203–65.

————— (2000), 'How Real is the Secular Decline in Rural Poverty?', *Economic and Political Weekly*, 35(25): 2129–40.

Townsend, P. (1979), 'The Development of Research on Poverty', *Social Security Research: The Definition and Measurement of Poverty*. London: Department of Health and Social Security, HMSO.

Townsend, P. (1985), 'A Sociological Approach to the Measurement of Poverty: A Rejoinder to Prof. Amartya Sen', *Oxford Economic Papers*, 37(4): 659–68.

———— (2004a), 'Basic Needs', in A. Kuper (ed.), *Social Sciences Encyclopaedia*. New York: Routledge.

Townsend, P. (2004b), 'Poverty', in Kuper (ed.), *Social Sciences Encyclopaedia*.

———— (2004c), 'Relative Deprivation', in Kuper (ed.), *Social Sciences Encyclopaedia*.

Watts, H. (1968), 'An Economic Definition of Poverty', in D.P. Moynihan (ed.), *On Understanding Poverty*. New York: Basic Books.

World Bank (1990), *World Development Report 1990*. Washington, D.C.: World Bank Press.

———— (2001), *World Development Report 2000/2001*. New York: Oxford University Press.

Index